BUSINESS PRACTICE

1

BUSINESS PRACTICE Series

Focuses on a variety of situations involved in business and provides opportunities to improve learners' communication skills in the workplace.

CARROT HOUSE

Business Practice 1
© Carrot House

All rights reserved. No part of this publication may be reproduced,
stored in a retrieval system, or transmitted in any form or by any means
without the prior permission in writing of Carrot House

Printed: March 2021
Author: Carrot Language Lab

ISBN 978-89-6732-116-1

Printed and distributed in Korea
9F, 488. Gangnam St, Gangnam-gu, Seoul, 06120, Korea

Curriculum Map

Course	Level 1	Level 2	Level 3	Level 4	Level 5	Level 6	Level 7	Text Book
General Conversation	Essential English: Begin Again							
	Pre Get Up to Speed 1~2	New Get Up to Speed+ 1~2						
			New Get Up to Speed+ 3~4					
				New Get Up to Speed+ 5~6				
					New Get Up to Speed+ 7~8			
	Daily Focused English 1							
		Daily Focused English 2						
Discussion			Active Discussion 1					
				Active Discussion 2				
					Dynamic Discussion			
			Chicken Soup Course					
				Dynamic Information & Digital Technology				
Business Conversation	Pre Business Basics 1							
		Pre Business Basics 2						
		Business Basics 1						
			Business Basics 2					
				Business Practice 1				
					Business Practice 2			
Global Biz Workshop			Effective Business Writing Skills (Workbook)					
			Effective Presentation Skills (Workbook)					
				Effective Negotiation Skills (Workbook)				
				Cross-Cultural Training 1~2 (Workbook)				
				Leadership Training Course (Workbook)				
Business Skills			Simple & Clear Technical Writing Skills					
			Effective Business Writing Skills					
			Effective Meeting Skills					
			Business Communication (Negotiation)					
			Effective Presentation Skills					
				Marketing 1				
					Marketing 2			
					Management			
On the Job English			Armed forces 1					
			Armed forces 2					
			Aviation 1					
			Aviation 2					
			English for Cabin Crew					
			English for Call Centers					
			English for Medical Professionals					
				English for Aviation Maintenance Technicians				

※ This Curriculum Map illustrates the entire line-up of textbooks at CARROT HOUSE.

CARROT HOUSE

Business Practice 1

Introduction

Carrot House Methodology

Andragogical Approach & Productive English

The teaching of children (pedagogy) and adult learning (andragogy) are distinctively different. Pedagogy is akin to training and encourages convergent thinking and rote learning. It is compulsory, centered on the teacher and the imparting of information with minimal control by the learner. Andragogy, by contrast, is about education as freedom. It encourages divergent thinking and active learning. It is voluntary, learner oriented and opens up vistas for continuing learning. Adults need to feel independent and in control of their learning. Therefore, Carrot House curriculum is based on andragogy and is designed to encourage learners' participation and engagement by providing more task-based activities and opportunities to frequently interact in the classroom.

People want to achieve communicative competence when they learn other languages. English education in EFL environments has been rather focused on the receptive skills of English—listening and reading—which simply increases learners' knowledge about a language, not the competence of using it. If people are well equipped with productive skills—speaking and writing—they will be competent in English communication.

This is why Carrot House curriculum is designed to enhance learners' productive skills throughout the course. This andragogical approach of the Carrot House Curriculum, which focuses on productive English, will enable learners to achieve communication skills necessary for global competence. Carrot House's teaching philosophy and curriculum combine to provide a "Language for Success" for all learners.

Communicative Language Learning (CLL)

This communicative interaction, the essential component of language acquisition, does not occur in a typical, non-meaningful, fun-oriented conversation with native speakers. It occurs in a negotiated interaction through which a well-trained teacher provides the comprehensible input that is appropriate to the learners. The learners, at the same time, actively utilize the opportunities given to them by the teachers.

To this end, the Communicative Language Learning (CLL) method is employed in the field of Foreign Language Acquisition. The CLL method provides activities that are geared toward using language pragmatically, authentically and functionally with the intention of achieving meaningful purposes.

Course Overview

I. Objectives

BUSINESS PRACTICE Series is designed to enhance learners' communication skills in the workplace by providing a wide range of situations involved in business. Each series is targeted at intermediate level learners. Through constant classroom interactions, learners can improve their productivity proficiency to achieve success in international transactional situations.

II. How to Use Business Practice 1

II-1 Lesson Composition

The book consists of 16 lessons (4 units) based on topics of great interest to everyone involved in business. The composition of each lesson is as below.

Learning Objectives
Set clear goals to acknowledge target learning of each lesson.
- Go over the learning objectives with learners to understand the learning focus.
- Review the objectives at the end of each lesson to reinforce each point.

Warm Up Activities
Stimulate learners' thinking and put them at ease in an English speaking environment through situation-related questions and role play.
- Open the class with discussions questions and encourage learners to brainstorm answers together.
- Pair up learners to look at the situation and role play.
- Encourage learners to express their own opinions regarding the questions and situations.

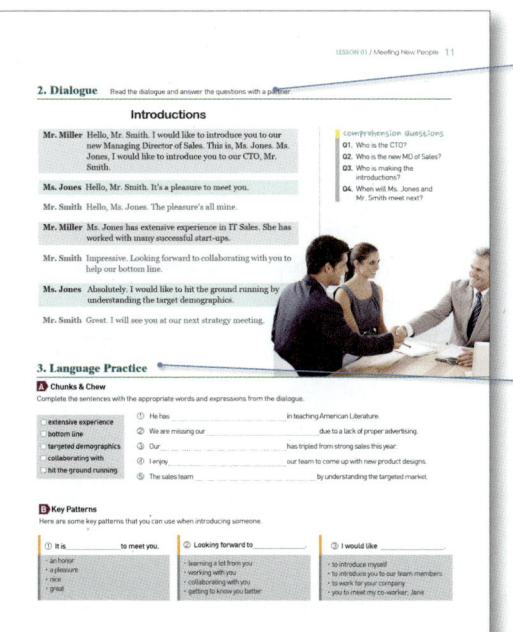

Dialogue
Role play the dialogue to practice English speaking in business situations. Help learners improve their comprehension skills and utilize useful expressions.
- Pair up class to practice the dialogue.
- Give feedback on each learner's role play.
- Allow learners' to answer the comprehension questions to review their understanding.

Language Practice
Reinforce useful chunks and patterns through substitution drills. Learners will practice how to use the essential expressions within their business lives.
- Have learners study the chunks and learn how to apply it in various situations.
- Have learners review chunks and key patterns by creating their own sentences.

Business Practice 1

Business Basics
Expand learners' ability to understand essential business skills.
- Have learners read the background information and check their understanding.
- Encourage learners to apply the business basics skills in real situations.

Role Plays
Reinforce learners' response skills in various business situations through role play activities. This will enable learners to apply the thematic situations and the skills of global business communication.
- Pair up class to review each situation.
- learners create dialogue and role play using the background information provided.
- Give feedback on each learner's role play.
- Each lesson has 3 situations to review.

Discussion
Provide opportunities to share learners' personal experience, ideas, and opinions in more depth.
- Pair up or form groups to discuss the questions provided.
- Allow learners' to present their ideas to each other.

One Point Lesson
Provides learners with language practice on commonly made expression or vocabulary errors.
- Learners review commonly made mistakes through reading the passage.
- To be used flexibly.

Business Skills
Expand learners' ability to develop essential business skills, such as making presentations, taking part in meetings, telephoning, and using English in social situations. Learners will learn business manners or etiquette through the medium of English.
- Have learners read the background information and complete the task as a pair or as group work.
- Encourage learners to practice 'good business manners and etiquette' through understanding and discussing the information provided.

Wrapping Up
Recall and review material learned each lesson by calling out words that instantly come to mind.
- Ask learners to call out words they remember from the lesson.
- Review why they recall those words in particular.

II-2 Case Studies

Each unit includes a Case Study. The Case Studies are based on realistic business situations and problems. They will encourage students to develop communication skills and problem solving skills by giving them opportunities to practice in realistic business situations.

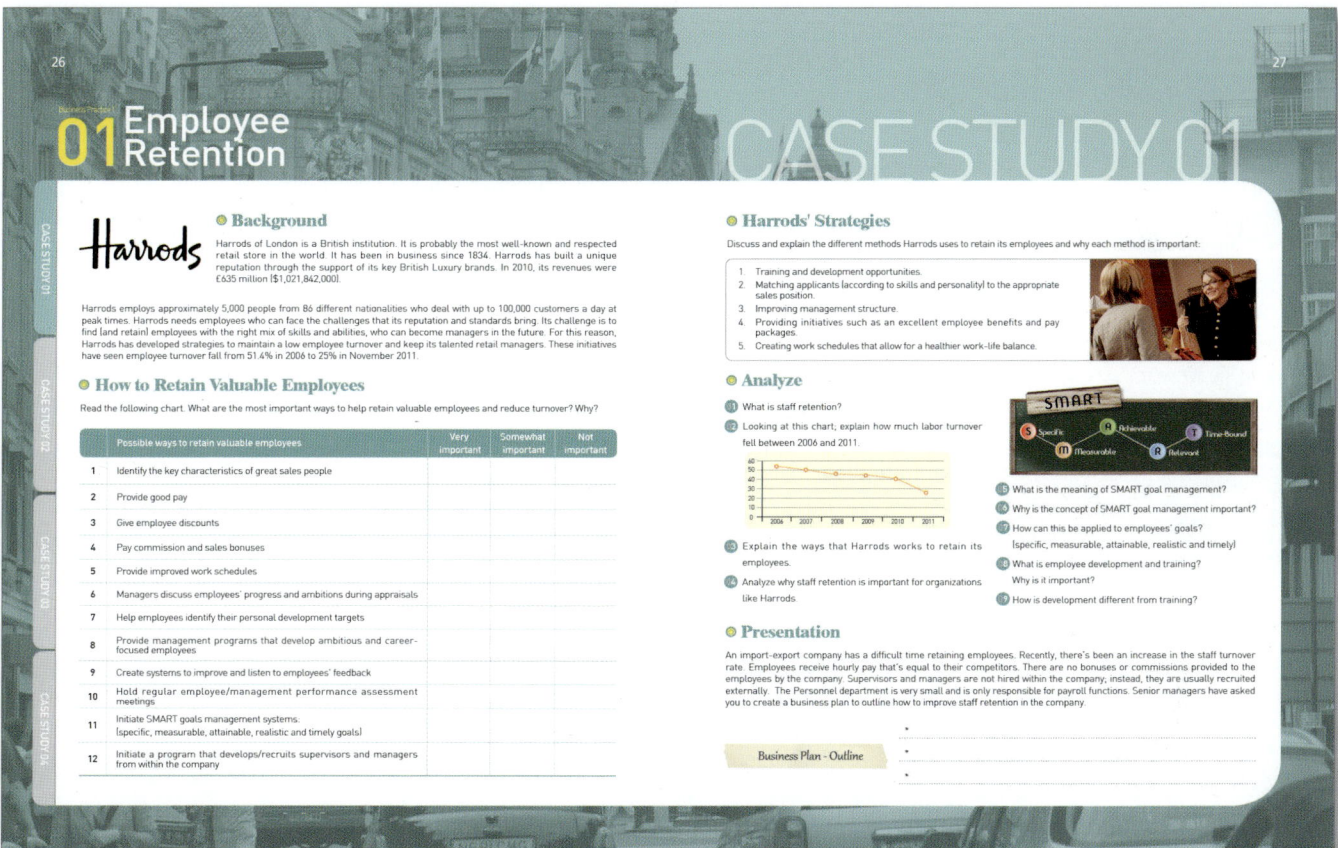

Background Information
Have learners read and understand background information about the company.

Discussion
Have learners complete an activity that encourages them to think about the problem the company faced and how the problem could be addressed.
- Pair up or form groups to talk about the problem.
- Ask learners to think about how the problem should be dealt with.

Analyze
Encourage learners to talk about the real strategies and how effective they were.
- Have learners read a short passage regarding the strategies the company adopted to solve problems.
- Ask learners questions related to the passage and discuss in more depth.

Presentation
Encourage learners to present their solutions as they would in real business situations.
- Allow individual or group work to present solutions, the logic behind the solutions, and their expected outcomes.

CONTENTS

Unit 1. People & Relationships

Lesson Title	Learning Objectives	Key Patterns	Business Skills	Page
Lesson 01 Meeting New People	- to introduce yourself or someone else - to ask and answer questions when meeting a person for the first time	· It is...to meet you. · Looking forward to... · I would like...	Showing Interest	10
Lesson 02 Socializing	- to have general conversation with your colleagues to establish a positive climate - to explain what business people usually do after work	· How is...treating you? · We were wondering if you... · I'll keep you posted (updated)...	Interactive Small Talk Strategies	14
Lesson 03 Working with International Visitors	- to work with overseas colleagues or clients and provide warm hospitality - to build good relations with your business partners	· Believe it or not,... · Would you take the time to...? · Since when...	Formal vs. Informal	18
Lesson 04 Building Teamwork	- to describe people and talk about co-workers at your workplace - to understand various types of colleagues and how to collaborate with them as a team	· I can't walk... through... · I'll let you know... · Would it be possible for you to...	Talking about Schedules	22
CASE STUDY	**[HARRODS]** Employee Retention * **Task**: To analyze the methods Harrods uses to retain its employees and why they are important * **Presentation**: To create a business plan to outline how to improve staff retention in a company			26

Unit 2. Company & Business

Lesson Title	Learning Objectives	Key Patterns	Business Skills	Page
Lesson 05 Introducing Your Company	- to present a detailed description of your company (company type and industry) - to effectively explain the products and services your company provides	· How do you like...? · To be honest with you,... · I'm responsible for...	Presentation Skills	28
Lesson 06 Work Environment	- to describe your working environment (e.g., working hours, facilities) - to ask questions and talk about business life (e.g., work and life balance)	· It seems... · What are the best ways...? · Why don't we...?	Describing Your Work Environment	32
Lesson 07 Following Company Policies	- to talk about your company's policies (e.g., dress code, smoking, personal calls) - to exchange opinions on your company's policies	· I'll make sure... · I've been trying to... · I'm supposed to...	Dress for Success	36
Lesson 08 Prospecting the Future	- to ask and answer questions about new products and their brands on the market - to compare different aspects of companies and assess your company's value	· That is one of the reasons... · ...soon after... · ...(be) heading to/for...	Questions about New Products	40
CASE STUDY	**[BALFOUR BEATTY CONSTRUCTION]** Focus on Sustainability * **Task**: To analyze the decrease of Balfour Beatty's construction projects in the US and the breakthrough by accomplishing sustainability * **Presentation**: To create a proposal response about how sustainability will affect a client's decision			44

Unit 3. Communicating in Business

Lesson Title	Learning Objectives	Key Patterns	Business Skills	Page
Lesson 09 Leaving a Message	- to talk on the phone and take or leave a message - to use appropriate telephone etiquette	· ...get/have (something) + *past participle*... · I appreciate... / I'd appreciate it if... · ...just to be sure.	Talking on the phone	46
Lesson 10 Making Arrangements	- to make arrangements with other people - to select an ideal time and a place for a global meeting	· ...provide (someone) with... · Would (someone) be able to...? · ...get back to (somebody)...	Scheduling a Meeting	50
Lesson 11 Exchanging Opinions	- to express your opinions effectively and make suggestions - to brainstorm various ideas and mildly disagree with assertions from other participants	· ...(be) in danger of... · It/That would be great... · I like how...	Interactive Meeting Skills	54
Lesson 12 Following Up	- to follow up plans after a meeting and develop a business relationship by e-mail - to make sure of what is discussed to follow up afterward	· ...(be) on the cutting edge... · ...(be) just being + *adjective* · Good luck in/on/with...	Following Up by E-mail	58
CASE STUDY	[WEB.COM] Outsourcing Customer Service * Task: To analyze barriers to communication that Web.com experienced after they outsourced their customer support * Presentation: To make a business plan to decrease problems due to cultural differences and deliver a presentation			62

Unit 4. Cross-Cultural Relations

Lesson Title	Learning Objectives	Key Patterns	Business Skills	Page
Lesson 13 Going on a Business Trip	- to plan a business trip and know how to book airline tickets and make hotel reservations - to know how to behave appropriately on a business trip	· Don't forget to... · To be frank,... · ...might not be available...	Business Trip & Business Etiquette	64
Lesson 14 Understanding Cultural Diversity	- to describe your overseas experience and cultural differences you've experienced - to get information about business culture and etiquette	· Now that... · ...make an appointment... · It isn't necessary to...	Cultural Diversity & Cultural Values	68
Lesson 15 Different Communication Styles	- to understand different communication styles depending on cultures - to avoid making cultural mistakes when communicating	· Did you hear...? · ...views (someone) as... · ...(be) chosen for...	Understanding Different Communication Styles	72
Lesson 16 Global Business Success	- to talk about global brands and the factors to succeed in the globalized market - to discuss the close relationship between understanding cultures and doing business internationally	· By the time... · Have you ever...? · ...(be/be not) *adjective* + enough...	Global Brands & Success	76
CASE STUDY	[CHEVRON TEXACO] Embrace Diversity * Task: To analyze the cross-cultural training courses Chevron Texaco adopts for their employees who have various cultural backgrounds * Writing: To write a business e-mail addressing how to improve relations between international employees			80

Lesson 01
Meeting New People

Learning Objectives
After completing this lesson, you will be able to...
- introduce yourself or someone else.
- ask and answer questions when meeting a person for the first time.

OVERVIEW
- ☐ Warm Up Activities
- ☐ Useful Expressions
- ☐ Dialogue
- ☐ Language Practice
- ☐ Business Basics
- ☐ Role Plays
- ☐ Discussion
- ☐ One Point Lesson
- ☐ Business Skills
- ☐ Business Manner & Etiquette

1. Warm Up Activities

A Discuss the following questions with a partner.
1. When you meet new people at work, do you usually bow or shake hands?
2. When you give your business card, do you give it with two hands or with one hand?
3. What kind of questions do you ask to get to know someone at work?

B Today's situation
Look at the situation and role play with your classmates.

> "What if you have to introduce someone?"

There are three people listed below.
Mr. Miller needs to introduce Ms. Jones to Mr. Smith.

- ⓐ Mr. Miller
- ⓑ Ms. Jones (a new Managing Director of Sales)
- ⓒ Mr. Smith (a Chief Technology Officer)

Useful Expressions

A When you are introducing yourself / someone else

ⓐ Nice to meet you. I'm Jerry.
ⓑ I'm Susan. It's nice to meet you, too!

ⓐ I don't think we've met. My name is Jerry.
ⓑ Hi, Jerry! I'm George.

ⓐ Janette, this is Mike. Mike, this is Janette.
ⓑ I'm happy to finally meet you.

ⓐ Tom, I'd like you to meet my co-worker, James.
ⓑ So glad to meet you James. You can call me Tommy.

ⓐ I'll introduce you around the office.
ⓑ Thank you for your kindness.

B When you cannot remember someone's name

* Excuse me. I didn't catch your name. Would you please repeat your name?
* May I have your name again?
* Could you spell your first name? That will help me pronounce it better.

LESSON 01 / Meeting New People 11

2. Dialogue
Read the dialogue and answer the questions with a partner.

Introductions

Mr. Miller Hello, Mr. Smith. I would like to introduce you to our new Managing Director of Sales. This is, Ms. Jones. Ms. Jones, I would like to introduce you to our CTO, Mr. Smith.

Ms. Jones Hello, Mr. Smith. It's a pleasure to meet you.

Mr. Smith Hello, Ms. Jones. The pleasure's all mine.

Mr. Miller Ms. Jones has extensive experience in IT Sales. She has worked with many successful start-ups.

Mr. Smith Impressive. Looking forward to collaborating with you to help our bottom line.

Ms. Jones Absolutely. I would like to hit the ground running by understanding the target demographics.

Mr. Smith Great. I will see you at our next strategy meeting.

Comprehension Questions
Q1. Who is the CTO?
Q2. Who is the new MD of Sales?
Q3. Who is making the introductions?
Q4. When will Ms. Jones and Mr. Smith meet next?

3. Language Practice

A Chunks & Chew
Complete the sentences with the appropriate words and expressions from the dialogue.

- ☐ extensive experience
- ☐ bottom line
- ☐ targeted demographics
- ☐ collaborating with
- ☐ hit the ground running

① He has _____ in teaching American Literature.
② We are missing our _____ due to a lack of proper advertising.
③ Our _____ has tripled from strong sales this year.
④ I enjoy _____ our team to come up with new product designs.
⑤ The sales team _____ by understanding the targeted market.

B Key Patterns
Here are some key patterns that you can use when introducing someone.

① It is _____ to meet you.
- an honor
- a pleasure
- nice
- great

② Looking forward to _____.
- learning a lot from you
- working with you
- collaborating with you
- getting to know you better

③ I would like _____.
- to introduce myself
- to introduce you to our team members
- to work for your company
- you to meet my co-worker, Jane

Business Basics

A. Understanding Corporate Hierarchy

The highest level officers in a company or corporation are C-level.

- **CEO**, Chief Executive Officer
- **CEM**, Chief Executive Manager for US LLC (limited liability corporation)
- **COO**, Chief Operations Officer, or **CPO**, Chief Program Officer (government)
- **CFO**, Chief Financial Officer
- **CTO**, Chief Technology Officer

B. Who is the most important person there?

When you have to introduce two people to each other, you should consider who the more important person is. Suppose that Peter Smith is a client of your company, and Kelly Clark is a co-worker.

e.g.
"Mr. Peter Smith, I'd like to introduce you to Kelly Clark, our West-coast manager. (Looking at Kelly Clark) Mr. Smith is our new client and it's his first time in San Diego."

4. Role Plays

Read each situation and role play with your partner.

01 Situation
You are the leader of the marketing department and have a new staff member. Now introduce him/her to the other leaders of the company.

02 Situation
You have a meeting with your client. You visit the office with a new colleague who joined a few months ago. You need to introduce your colleague to the client and vice versa.

03 Situation
At a conference, you meet Jeff Hancock who is a client of your company and Jack Wood, one of your co-workers. You want to introduce them to each other.

5. Discussion

Discuss the following questions in detail.

1. What is considered appropriate to ask when meeting a new colleague for the very first time? What is regarded as inappropriate?
2. When meeting a colleague for the first time, what do you consider?
3. How do you treat superiors versus subordinates in your office when greeting them?
4. Does age play a factor when greeting colleagues?

One Point Lesson

Collaboration vs. Cooperation

 "The police were grateful to the public for their collaboration."

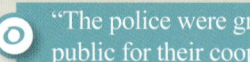 "The police were grateful to the public for their cooperation."

Collaboration comes from the verb "collaborate," which means **"to work in partnership with someone on the same task."** When collaborating, people work together on a single shared goal, like an orchestra, which follows a script everyone has agreed upon, while each musician plays his or her part not for its own sake but to help make something bigger. Meanwhile, cooperation comes from the verb "cooperate," which means **"to be willing to help someone to achieve something; be helpful."**

LESSON 01 / Meeting New People   13

6. Business Skills - Showing Interest

Learn how to show your interest in the conversation and continue it effectively.

A. Read the dialogue and discuss the problem.

Situation: Rick takes part in an international conference as a representative of his company. He sees Debbie and decides he would like to get to know her.

Rick	Hello. Where are you from?
Debbie	I'm from New York.
Rick	What made you come to the conference?
Debbie	To work.
Rick	Oh, which company do you work for?
Debbie	IT company.
Rick	How long do you plan to stay here?
Debbie	Just two weeks.
Rick	When did you get here?
Debbie	A week ago.

What's the problem?
_____
_____

B. Change the conversation by adding questions or comments to their short answers.

Rick	Hello. Where are you from?
Debbie	I'm from New York. _____
Rick	_____
	What made you come to the conference?
Debbie	To work. _____
Rick	_____
	Oh, which company do you work for?
Debbie	IT company. _____
Rick	_____
	How long do you plan to stay here?
Debbie	Just two weeks. _____
Rick	_____
	When did you get here?
Debbie	A week ago.

Business Manner & Etiquette

The Proper Handshake

Handshakes are the universally accepted business greeting. You could be judged by the quality of your handshake. The following are guidelines to having a good handshake.

- Maintain eye contact
- Keep the handshake firm but painless
- Hold the handshake about three seconds
- Give only two or three pumps
- Start and stop crisply
- Do not shake hands through the entire introduction
- Keep your fingers together and your thumb up
- Slide the web of your hand all the way to the web of the other person's hand. Otherwise, he or she ends up shaking hands with your fingers.

Wrapping Up!

▶ 3 new words from this lesson
_____
_____
_____

▶ 3 new expressions from this lesson
_____
_____
_____

▶ 3 things to remember
_____
_____
_____

Lesson 02
Socializing

Learning Objectives
After completing this lesson, you will be able to...
- have general conversations with your colleagues to establish a positive climate.
- explain what business people usually do after work.

OVERVIEW
- ☐ Warm Up Activities
- ☐ Useful Expressions
- ☐ Dialogue
- ☐ Language Practice
- ☐ Business Basics
- ☐ Role Plays
- ☐ Discussion
- ☐ One Point Lesson
- ☐ Business Skills
- ☐ Business Manner & Etiquette

1. Warm Up Activities

A Discuss the following questions with a partner.
1. How much do you socialize with people from work? What do you usually do with them?
2. How often do you go out to dinner with co-workers?
3. What questions should you ask when you first meet new team members?

B Today's situation
Look at the situation and role play with your classmates.

"I would like to invite someone to a social gathering."

Jenny was transferred to the New York office. She has worked for the first week at the office, and she is finally meeting Don, a co-worker she talked to on the phone a couple of times when she was in Beijing. Don would like to invite Jenny to a social gathering.

Useful Expressions

A Talking about weekend plans or after work

ⓐ What are you up to this weekend?
ⓑ I might go camping if the weather is nice.

ⓐ Do you have any plans for this weekend?
ⓑ I'm going to have a barbecue on Saturday.

ⓐ Why don't we go skiing on Saturday?
ⓑ Sounds like a plan. Where do you want to go?

ⓐ Let's go bowling tonight.
ⓑ Sorry, I can't. I'm meeting a friend for dinner.

B Asking work-related questions

Match the expressions (1-4) with the similar meanings (a-d).

① How is work treating you?
② I'll brief my crew and keep you posted.
③ I've fallen behind on the project.
④ I had hectic days all this week.

☐ a. I failed to finish the project on time.
☐ b. How's work going for you?
☐ c. I've been tied up this week.
☐ d. I'll inform my co-workers first and will keep you updated.

2. Dialogue

Read the dialogue and answer the questions with a partner.

Invitation to a Social Gathering

Don   Hi, you must be Jenny from the Beijing office. Please come in.

Jenny   Mr. Jones? It's nice to finally meet you. I will be working on your team for the next six months.

Don   Oh, just call me Don. How is your first week in New York treating you?

Jenny   I've been all tied up with catching up on the newly-assigned project. I've fallen behind, but other than that, everything's going great. Everyone in the office is friendly and nice, and they are all patient with me.

Don   That's great! By the way, we were wondering if you had plans for this Friday night. We've been talking about this Japanese style bar that just opened a week ago, and we decided to check it out on Friday.

Jenny   I'd be delighted. Thank you.

Don   Great. I'll brief my crew and keep you posted if there are any changes.

Jenny   Likewise.

Comprehension Questions

Q1. How long has Jenny been working in New York?
Q2. Why did Don call Jenny into his office?
Q3. What are the co-workers' plans for this Friday night?
Q4. Why are they planning to check out the Japanese bar?

3. Language Practice

A. Chunks & Chew

Complete the sentences with the appropriate words and expressions from the dialogue.

- ☐ catching up on
- ☐ fallen behind on (with)
- ☐ check out
- ☐ keep / posted
- ☐ brief / on

① I was there .... some accounts.
② .... the new comedy show on tonight!
③ Can you .... me .... what happened at the meeting yesterday?
④ They had .... their mortgage repayments.
⑤ It's your job to .... me .... on what's going on around the office.

B. Key Patterns

Here are some key patterns that you can use when socializing with your co-workers.

① How is _____ treating you?	· school · work · life · London
② We were wondering if you _____.	· had plans next Friday · wanted to go out for drinks after work · had gotten the results yet
③ I'll keep you posted (updated) _____.	· of all the events that are happening this year · on what needs to be done by Sunday · if there are any changes

Business Basics

Small Talk for Successful Business

Small talk might be about nothing important, but small talk itself is important. Being able to make small talk allows you to make yourself part of a group.

I. Goal of Small Talk
We engage in small talk to show friendliness and openness and to make people comfortable before business or a serious conversation begins. Silence is not comfortable in many Western cultures. In the UK, small talk is an essential preamble to business talk.

II. Common Topics
We normally look at more common topics for small talk, such as the weather, current social issues, or events which happened to the acquaintances.

III. Exit Thoughtfully
Find an appropriate point in the conversation to make an exit. You can use the following expressions to express pleasure at the conversation:
"It was nice talking to you" or "I really enjoyed talking to you."

Then, you show regret at the upcoming separation:
"I'm sorry I can't talk longer. I'll be in touch with you later so we can discuss it further. I'll see you."

4. Role Plays

Read each situation and role play with your partner.

01 Situation
You arrive at a morning strategic meeting 10 minutes early. A few people are already there. You say hello and make small talk with a person sitting next to you.

02 Situation
You are attending a meeting in Chicago. While flying, you happen to sit by a British businessman who is currently working in Chicago. Strike up a conversation with the person in the seat next to you.

03 Situation
You are invited to a conference in Europe. You are also invited to a drinks reception after the conference. It is such a great opportunity for you to meet with professionals from all over the world. You meet a person who is a well-known and recognized expert in your industry and want to have a conversation with him/her.

5. Discussion

Discuss the following questions in detail.

1. What are some business socializing rules (with your colleagues/clients/bosses) in your country?
2. Do you easily strike up conversations with strangers at conferences?
3. Have you ever been in charge of planning an event with clients or team members?
4. A "business lunch" is one of the ways to develop relationships. What are some general rules for a successful meeting?

One Point Lesson

Fun vs. Funny

ⓧ Learning English is very funny.
◯ Learning English is great fun.

Fun and funny are two words that are often confused due to the similarity between their connotations. The word "funny" is used in the sense of "hilarious." It is used for someone or something that makes us laugh. For example, we can say, "I always laugh at his jokes. They are really funny." On the other hand, the word "fun" is used in the sense of "enjoyment." It is used for someone or something that gives you pleasure or enjoyment. We can say, "The Disneyland trip sounds like a lot of fun."

LESSON 02 / Socializing   17

6. Business Skills – Interactive Small Talk Strategies

Do you want to build a good relationship by creating small talk? If you want to socialize well, you need to learn interactive small talk strategies.

A Categorizing

Look at list of expressions and fill in the blanks of the correct category.

List of Expressions	Category
☐ All over the country?	**1) Showing Interest**
☐ How did you feel?	* Uh-huh. I understand.
☐ Neither do I.	*
✓ Uh-huh. I understand.	*
☐ So, what happened to you?	**2) Finding Common Areas**
☐ Absolutely. I agree.	*
☐ Then, what did you do next?	*
☐ That sounds interesting!	*
☐ Really?	**3) Further Questions**
☐ Born in England?	*
☐ So do I.	*
☐ Three thousand?	*
	4) Echoing Interesting Facts
	*
	*
	*

B How to Respond

What would you say if a person said each phrase below? Write a proper response showing interest.

a. "I want to move to Russia to live the rest of my life."

Your response would be...

b. "I missed the bus this morning, and I was 15 minutes late to work."

Your response would be...

c. "Did you hear that? Lisa went into the hospital again."

Your response would be...

d. "I think Sophie should have told the truth to her supervisor."

Your response would be...

Wrapping Up!

▶ 3 new words from this lesson

▶ 3 new expressions from this lesson

▶ 3 things to remember

Business Manner & Etiquette
Table Manners - Napkin Etiquette

Using the napkin correctly shows confidence, good manners, and attention to details, which are valued traits in business encounters.

		Yes	No
01	In a banquet setting or at a restaurant, place your napkin on your lap as soon as you are seated.	Yes	No
02	Lightly press your napkin around your mouth to dab any liquid or food.	Yes	No
03	Clean the cutlery or wipe your face with the napkin.	Yes	No
04	If you are afraid of spilling something during the meal, it is better to tuck the napkin into your shirt like a bib to protect your shirt from spills.	Yes	No
05	When you need to excuse yourself, place the napkin on the table.	Yes	No
06	When you finish your meal, place the napkin on the left of the dessert plate.	Yes	No

* Answers: 1) Yes 2) Yes 3) No 4) No 5) No (Place the napkin on the chair.) 6) Yes

Lesson 03
Working with International Visitors

Learning Objectives
After completing this lesson, you will be able to...
- work with overseas colleagues or clients and provide warm hospitality.
- build good relations with your business partners.

OVERVIEW
- ☐ Warm Up Activities
- ☐ Useful Expressions
- ☐ Dialogue
- ☐ Language Practice
- ☐ Business Basics
- ☐ Role Plays
- ☐ Discussion
- ☐ One Point Lesson
- ☐ Business Skills
- ☐ Business Manner & Etiquette

1. Warm Up Activities

A Discuss the following questions with a partner.

1. Have you ever been in charge of planning an event for overseas colleagues/clients?
2. How often do you take overseas guests out for dinner? What dishes would you recommend to the visitors?
3. Have you ever had problems getting along with overseas colleagues?

B Today's situation

Look at the situation and role play with your classmates.

"You are having an overseas visitor today!"

Steve, the overseas client, is visiting the office to attend the annual conference. He is also very keen on checking out the introduction of a new line of products. He just arrived yesterday from Canada. Don is in charge of welcoming and explaining about the conference.

Useful Expressions

A When you ask something about the visitor's country

ⓐ What is the traffic like in Beijing?
ⓑ It is terrible, especially during rush hour.

ⓐ What is the weather like in Tokyo?
ⓑ Tokyo is a fairly temperate city with a climate that is seasonal.

B When you have a conversation with overseas visitors

Match the expressions (1-4) with the similar meanings (a-d).

① If time permits, I'll see you after the meeting.
② Right off the bat, I knew I was going to get along with her.
③ We're pressed for time, so we'd better get going now.
④ You can easily spot them from a distance.

a. It is easy to recognize them although we're a long way away from them.
b. We're running out of time, so it's better that we leave now.
c. If it finishes early enough, I'll be able to see you after the meeting.
d. I immediately knew I was going to have a good relationship with her.

2. Dialogue
Read the dialogue and answer the questions with a partner.

Welcoming Overseas Clients

Don Steve, it's so good to see you again. How was the flight?

Steve It was great. I'm still jet-lagged, though.

Don Oh no, hope you feel better soon. So, you're here to attend the annual conference this time?

Steve Also, if time permits, I'd like to check out the Food and Beverage Exhibition.

Don Oh yeah? We are planning to introduce our new organic dressings at the exhibition.

Steve Believe it or not, that's also why I decided to make the trip to New York. This may even turn out to be a great opportunity to meet new potential partners.

Don Take a look around. Let me know if there's anything I can do to help.

Steve Well, right off the bat, I like how you can easily spot the new products in the hallway displays.

Don Thank you for saying that. We decided to go with hallway displays because we are kind of pressed for space. Any questions regarding the conference?

Steve Would you take the time to introduce the new products in the conference as well?

Don We'd like to if we weren't so pressed for time. Since when have you been on such a health kick? You seem very keen on organic products.

Steve Since the bean counters crunched the numbers and found that we could save a lot by bringing in a new product line.

Don Okay, you're the boss. Tell me what needs to be done before you return to Canada.

Comprehension Questions
- **Q1.** What is the purpose of Steve's visit to New York?
- **Q2.** What is Steve's take on bringing a new product line to the market?
- **Q3.** How does Don respond to Steve's request?

3. Language Practice

A Chunks & Chew
Complete the sentences with the appropriate words and expressions from the dialogue.

- ☐ right off the bat
- ☐ bean counters
- ☐ (be) pressed for
- ☐ crunched the numbers
- ☐ on a health kick

① If you're _____ space, you might want to get a sofa bed.
② The guy _____ before he gave me a price.
③ The _____ refused to authorize the costs.
④ I could tell _____ that she wasn't happy.
⑤ You have really been _____ lately.

B Key Patterns
Here are some key patterns that you can use when working with international visitors.

① **Believe it or not,** _____.
- she is in her late 50s
- he asked me to marry him
- I'm reluctant to lead others at work

② **Would you take the time to** _____?
- read the directions carefully
- master the skills
- complete the survey

③ **Since when** _____?
- has it been such a big deal to you
- is he a leader
- did you start closing so early

Business Basics

Successful Business Lunch Strategy

I. Are You a Host?

If you are the host and arrange the meeting, you need to act that way by handling the bill and making sure your guest is comfortable, even when making menu recommendations. It is also good to let the server know the bill should come to you at the end of the meal.

II. Things to Consider before the Day!

Before you make a reservation for a restaurant, you need to consider whether the visitor is a smoker or not. In addition, be sure to find out whether your visitor is a vegetarian or has any food allergies. If you don't know the preferences of the person, don't choose an exotic or ethnic restaurant.

III. Don't Forget Why You Have a Business Lunch

People sometimes forget about the purpose of a meeting when they introduce food into the equation. Clearly state the purpose of the meeting. Never make it seem as if you want to take the person to lunch to thank him for something or simply as a social get-together.

4. Role Plays

Read each situation and role play with your partner.

It's Monday, and you have overseas visitors for the whole week. You need to explain how to use the facilities on the floor. For example, you need to show them the location of the conference room, elevators, restrooms, the main lobby, reception, and other places or facilities they can use.

Your boss has planned to take overseas partners out for dinner and drinks. However, your boss has been feeling under the weather all day and ended up asking you to show them around your office instead. Call and tell the partners about the changed schedule.

An international visitor visits your office and will stay until next Monday. It's Friday, and the visitor asks you to recommend a great place to go on the weekend as well as some good traditional dishes to enjoy.

5. Discussion

Discuss the following questions in detail.

1. Have you ever thought about working abroad as part of an overseas transfer?
2. What are some differences between local corporate culture and international corporate culture?
3. What role does corporate culture play in global business success?
4. What are some communication problems you have faced at work?
5. What are some good tips and strategies for impressing an important business client to maintain positive relationships while working together?

One Point Lesson

Opportunity vs. Chance

There is an opportunity that David's father will come tonight.

There is a chance that David's father will come tonight.

When you talk about the likelihood of something happening, use the word "chance." It usually refers to a neutral event that has some uncertainty attached to it: "there's a chance of rain later today." Chance is a favorable opportunity that comes seemingly by good fortune or accident and calls for action.

On the other hand, "opportunity" tends to refer to the possibility of doing something that benefits you. It implies an occurrence of circumstances favorable to doing something, especially something that corresponds to one's wishes, purposes, or inclinations.

6. Business Skills - Formal vs. Informal

People use formal English in academic writing such as; essays, reports, resumes, thesis, and public speeches at formal social events. Informal English is suitable for ordinary conversations or letters to friends. It is more used in everyday speech than in writing. The followings are examples.

Informal	VS	Formal
I'm sorry, but… I'm happy to say that…		We regret to inform you that… We have pleasure in announcing that…

A. Dictionary of Formal & Informal English

Fill in the blanks with the formal words which have the same meanings.

About	Regarding
And	
Because	
But	
Get in touch	
Enough	
Thanks	
Sorry	

B. Rewrite the Sentences

Read the following sentences and then rewrite them in a more polite and formal way.

a. How about dinner Saturday?

b. See you at the conference next Monday!

c. I want to have a meeting with you sometime next week.

d. You can call me any time.

e. I want to visit your new office. Is that okay?

f. I can't come to the trade fair next Monday. I'm busy.

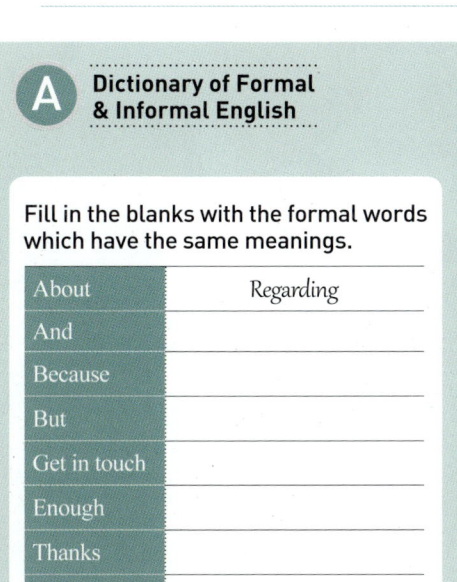
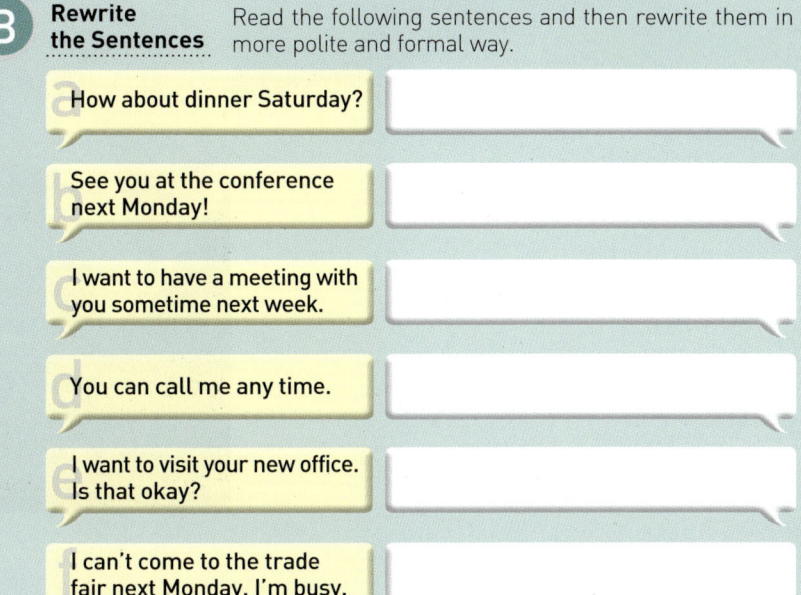

General Rules of Thumb for Asian Business Card Etiquette

The Asian culture has influenced the world in how we give, receive, use, and keep business cards. They believe the business card is an extension of introducing yourself on paper.

- Exchange your business card with two hands (as a sign of respect) or with your right hand, one-by-one, individual-to-individual.

- Business cards tend to represent the person to whom you are being introduced, so take a few moments to review and study the card.

- Turn your card right side up, so the other person can read it without needing to turn it over.

- Never immediately shove a business card into your back trouser or shirt pocket.

- Never write comments on another person's business card in their presence. Some countries believe that it is like writing on the person's face.

Wrapping Up!

▶ 3 new words from this lesson

▶ 3 new expressions from this lesson

▶ 3 things to remember

Lesson 04
Building Teamwork

Learning Objectives
After completing this lesson, you will be able to...
- describe people and talk about co-workers at your workplace.
- understand various types of colleagues and how to collaborate with them as a team.

OVERVIEW
☐ Warm Up Activities
☐ Useful Expressions
☐ Dialogue
☐ Language Practice
☐ Business Basics
☐ Role Plays
☐ Discussion
☐ One Point Lesson
☐ Business Skills
☐ Business Manner & Etiquette

1. Warm Up Activities

A Discuss the following questions with a partner.

1. Do you consider yourself to be mostly a team player or more of an individual contributor?
2. Have you ever worked with others to achieve a goal?
3. What are the advantages and disadvantages of working within a team?

B Today's situation

Look at the situation and role play with your classmates.

"When you prepare a meeting with team members."

Larry asks Rick and Jon to prepare for the meeting tomorrow morning. They need to get it done by the end of today. Jon will assist Rick while he structures the meeting plans.

Larry: Senior Manager, has 10 years experience
Rick: A Staff Member, joined the company 2 years ago
Jon: A Staff Member, has been working for the last 6 months

Useful Expressions

A Having a Team Meeting

Match the expressions (1-4) with the similar meanings (a-d).

① Let's get him on the horn and have him give us some ideas.
② Can you take the lead on the project?
③ Please don't fret over/about being a few minutes late.
④ I walked everyone through what to do during the ceremony

☐ a. Can you take charge of the project?
☐ b. I instructed everyone carefully, one step at a time.
☐ c. Let's call him on the phone to get some ideas.
☐ d. Don't worry too much about being a little late.

B Reacting to Suggestions

ⓐ Can you outline the presentation before getting started?
ⓑ (Positively) Sure. That sounds great.

ⓐ Why don't you give us an alternative proposal?
ⓑ (Neutrally) We could possibly do that.
 (My boss will have to check off on it first.)

ⓐ How about if we lower the price for this quarter?
ⓑ (Negatively) I'm afraid that we can't accept that.

2. Dialogue

Read the dialogue and answer the questions with a partner.

Meeting Preparations

Larry Jon, we should be well-prepared for the meeting tomorrow morning. Would it be possible for you to take the lead on the meeting planning?

Jon Sure. What should be my focus this time? Am I going to be working on a team?

Larry Yes, you'll get assistance from Rick. By the way, is Rick late again this morning?

Jon Speak of the devil. (Rick just walks in the door.)

Rick Hey, sorry I'm late. You wouldn't believe the traffic! What have you guys been talking about?

Larry Well, we've been working on tomorrow's meeting agenda. I have another meeting scheduled for tomorrow morning. I can't walk you through every detail this time, but I'll try to carry you through the highlights.

Jon Then, can you identify our minimum requirements before we get started?

Larry I'll let you know after getting Ted on the horn for some updates. Why don't you focus on the third quarter first because we at least expect things to pick back up in the third quarter?

Jon I'll do the math and see if it is feasible.

Larry Great. Please let me know by the end of today. Don't fret over every small detail. We don't have time for it.

Comprehension Questions

Q1. What does "speak of the devil" mean in this context?
Q2. Who is going to assist Jon while he structures the meeting preparation?
Q3. When does the meeting preparation need to be done by?
Q4. Does Jon seem confident in what he's being asked to do?

3. Language Practice

A Chunks & Chew

Complete the sentences with the appropriate words and expressions from the dialogue.

- ☐ speak of the devil
- ☐ get assistance from
- ☐ get / on the horn
- ☐ pick back up
- ☐ fret over

① I want you to _____ him _____ now.
② I sure hope sales will _____ soon, or we're really going to be in trouble.
③ Don't _____ your kids' weird habits!
④ Apparently she went there and wasn't that impressed – oh _____ here she is!
⑤ The visitors _____ the local agency.

B Key Patterns

Here are some key patterns that you can use when communicating with your team members.

① I can't walk _____ through _____.
- you / all the steps
- everyone / the changed company policies
- the staff / what to do whenever they make mistakes

② I'll let you know _____.
- when I get there
- if I come up with any other ideas
- when I receive a message from him

③ Would it be possible for you to _____?
- send the package to me
- provide the serial number for the gadget
- guide me through the process

Business Basics

Three Qualities of Effective Team Players

☐ **Communicate constructively**
Effective team players speak up and express their thoughts and ideas clearly, directly, honestly, and with respect for others and for the work of the team. Such a team member does not shy away from making a point but makes it in the best way possible in a positive, confident, and respectful manner.

☐ **Be active participants**
Good team players are active participants. They do not sit passively on the sideline. They are fully engaged in the work of the team. Such a team member takes the initiative to help make things happen.

☐ **Cooperate and pitch in to help**
Despite their differences in style and perspective, good team players figure out ways to work together to solve problems and get work done. Team players with commitment look beyond their own piece of the work and care about the team's overall work.

4. Role Plays

Read each situation and role play with your partner.

01 Situation Your team has been working on this massive project for months. Team members have almost completed the project as the deadline is just around the corner. You are currently in charge of the team and the project. Make a suggestion to your team that you'd like to take them out to lunch/dinner to empower your team members.

02 Situation Your team is going to have an end-of-the-year party on your wedding anniversary, so you can't attend the party. Your team leader thinks that every team member should attend the party. Explain to your team leader why you won't be able to join the gathering.

03 Situation You have a lazy co-worker on your team. He/she is always late for work and always fails to meet deadlines. You've decided to swing by your former boss's office on your way home because you felt the need to talk to him for some suggestions.

5. Discussion

Discuss the following questions in detail.
1. Have you ever had difficulty working with a manager/supervisor?
2. If you've had a good boss, tell your classmates about him/her. What made your boss good? How did it impact you at work?
3. What are some tips and strategies for building a successful team?
4. Do you have good people skills? What are some interpersonal skills you need at work?
5. How do you demonstrate respect at work, especially when working on a project with a group of people?

One Point Lesson

Late vs. Lately

 "My car broke down, so I arrived at the conference lately."

 "My car broke down, so I arrived at the conference late."

Late and lately are commonly misused. Late is an adjective that means to arrive at a place past the time you had planned to. Lately is an adverb that means in recent times, recently, or "these days."

Lately vs. Recently

 "Lately someone told me that she went to Russia to study."

 "Recently someone told me that she went to Russia to study."

Both lately and recently refer to a period of time that begins in the past and continues until, now, the moment of speaking. However, recently is usually used to refer to a point in time. Lately is usually used with the present perfect tense. (e.g. "Have you seen either of them lately?")

6. Business Skills - Talking about Schedule

Business people frequently talk about their daily or weekly schedules, especially when they are on the same team and have a shared goal. Learn how to effectively update others about your schedule.

 A Time-related Expressions

Fill in the blanks with the appropriate phrases from the word box.

Word Box
ahead of time, be pressed for time, (right) on time, in the nick of time, behind schedule,

① having failed to do something by the appointed time:

② beforehand; before the announced time:

③ just before it is too late:

④ in a hurry, under time pressure:

⑤ punctual or punctually:

 B Assigned Role and Schedule

Using the expressions you learned, have a conversation in the situation provided.

[Situation]
There is a task force team which consists of four people. Each person has a certain role to prepare for an upcoming conference which will be held on October 27th. **Today is the 15th of October**. Talk about the schedule and the status of the project based on the table below.

Project: Preparing an annual conference
Conference Day: Oct. 27th

NAME	ROLE ASSIGNED	STATUS	DUE DATE
Jerry	* To check and update the list of clients	Done	Oct. 13th
	* To send the invitations to the clients	Deferred	
Jason	* To prepare hand-out materials	In progress	Oct. 17th
	* To prepare a presentation about our products	In progress	
John	* To arrange the location and food	Done	Oct. 15th
	* To outline the conference schedule	In progress	
Bradley	* To create a website the clients can register on	Deferred	Oct. 12th

How to Say "No!" Nicely

Business Manner & Etiquette

Sometimes, you meet situations when you have to politely decline a person's offer. Rejections can be difficult, especially when you care about the person. If you say "no" directly, that can be very rude for the other person. The following phrases give you some ways to say "no" nicely and politely.

- "**That's very kind of you, but** I really have to get back to the office."
- "**Thank you, but** I am in the middle of several other projects right now."
- "**I'm afraid I can't** handle the task."
- "**Sorry, but I don't particularly** like Indian food."

Wrapping Up!

▶ 3 new words from this lesson

▶ 3 new expressions from this lesson

▶ 3 things to remember

01 Employee Retention

Business Practice 1

Background

Harrods of London is a British institution. It is probably the most well-known and respected retail store in the world. It has been in business since 1834. Harrods has built a unique reputation through the support of its key British Luxury brands. In 2010, its revenues were £635 million ($1,021,842,000).

Harrods employs approximately 5,000 people from 86 different nationalities who deal with up to 100,000 customers a day at peak times. Harrods needs employees who can face the challenges that its reputation and standards bring. Its challenge is to find (and retain) employees with the right mix of skills and abilities, who can become managers in the future. For this reason, Harrods has developed strategies to maintain a low employee turnover and keep its talented retail managers. These initiatives have seen employee turnover fall from 51.4% in 2006 to 25% in November 2011.

How to Retain Valuable Employees

Read the following chart. What are the most important ways to help retain valuable employees and reduce turnover? Why?

	Possible ways to retain valuable employees	Very important	Somewhat important	Not important
1	Identify the key characteristics of great sales people			
2	Provide good pay			
3	Give employee discounts			
4	Pay commission and sales bonuses			
5	Provide improved work schedules			
6	Managers discuss employees' progress and ambitions during appraisals			
7	Help employees identify their personal development targets			
8	Provide management programs that develop ambitious and career-focused employees			
9	Create systems to improve and listen to employees' feedback			
10	Hold regular employee/management performance assessment meetings			
11	Initiate SMART goals management systems: (specific, measurable, attainable, realistic and timely goals)			
12	Initiate a program that develops/recruits supervisors and managers from within the company			

CASE STUDY 01

◉ Harrods' Strategies

Discuss and explain the different methods Harrods uses to retain its employees and why each method is important:

1. Training and development opportunities.
2. Matching applicants (according to skills and personality) to the appropriate sales position.
3. Improving management structure.
4. Providing initiatives such as an excellent employee benefits and pay packages.
5. Creating work schedules that allow for a healthier work-life balance.

◉ Analyze

01 What is staff retention?

02 Looking at this chart; explain how much labor turnover fell between 2006 and 2011.

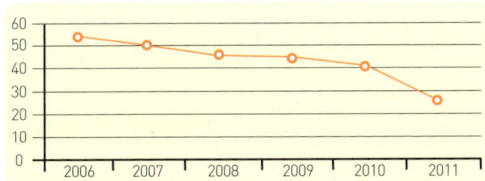

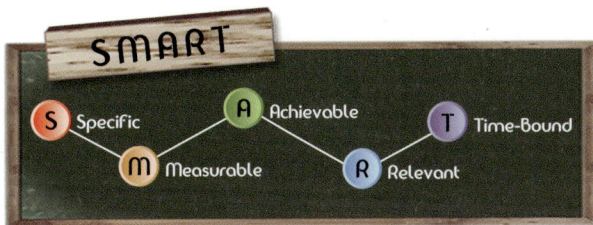

03 Explain the ways that Harrods works to retain its employees.

04 Analyze why staff retention is important for organizations like Harrods.

05 What is the meaning of SMART goal management?

06 Why is the concept of SMART goal management important?

07 How can this be applied to employees' goals? (specific, measurable, attainable, realistic and timely)

08 What is employee development and training? Why is it important?

09 How is development different from training?

◉ Presentation

An import-export company has a difficult time retaining employees. Recently, there's been an increase in the staff turnover rate. Employees receive hourly pay that's equal to their competitors. There are no bonuses or commissions provided to the employees by the company. Supervisors and managers are not hired within the company; instead, they are usually recruited externally. The Personnel department is very small and is only responsible for payroll functions. Senior managers have asked you to create a business plan to outline how to improve staff retention in the company.

Business Plan - Outline

* ....
* ....
* ....

Lesson 05
Introducing Your Company

Learning Objectives

After completing this lesson, you will be able to...
- present a detailed description of your company. (company type and industry)
- effectively explain the products and services your company provides.

OVERVIEW

☐ Warm Up Activities
☐ Useful Expressions
☐ Dialogue
☐ Language Practice
☐ Business Basics
☐ Role Plays
☐ Discussion
☐ One Point Lesson
☐ Business Skills

1. Warm Up Activities

A Discuss the following questions with a partner.

1. What kinds of products and services does your company provide?
2. What are your responsibilities at work?
3. In which countries does your company operate? Does your company have overseas branches?

B Today's situation

Look at the situation and role play with your classmates.

"When You Talk about Yourself and Your Company"

Todd and Judy ran into each other and struck up a conversation about Judy's new job. Judy just landed a better job a few weeks ago. The pay is good, and she gets great perks; however, she's not happy because she has to work extremely hard.

Useful Expressions

A Talking About You and Your Company

Match the expressions (1-4) with the similar meanings (a-d).

① I'm mainly responsible for overseeing construction projects.
② I just joined a new company.
③ I'm working in the sales department.
④ I'm going to get some good perks with my new job.

☐ a. I'm assigned to oversee construction projects.
☐ b. I just landed a new job.
☐ c. My company is going to offer good benefits for the employees.
☐ d. I'm in sales.

B Presenting Your Company

- The company is **based in** New York.
- **The head office is in** London.
- Our subsidiary/factory is **located in** Tokyo.

C Products and Services

- The company **specializes in** graphic design.
- **Our main products are** mobile phones.
- We **manufacture** and sell cosmetic products.

2. Dialogue
Read the dialogue and answer the questions with a partner.

Landing a New Job

Todd Hey, Judy. I can't believe I bumped into you! How are things with you?

Judy Pretty good!

Todd Susan tells me you just joined a new company. How do you like it so far?

Judy To be honest with you, it's been pretty tough. I worked freelance before I moved to this company. I'm currently working in the Sales Department. We sell software to small businesses. I'm mainly responsible for resolving customer complaints by investigating problems and also working on two other projects at the same time.

Todd Seriously?

Judy Yeah, but I'm getting a pay hike with great perks. Overall, it's not too bad, but I still miss having more flexible hours sometimes.

Todd Yeah, well, you can't have your cake and eat it, too. So, tell me more about your company. How many people are working there?

Judy It's a New York-based company that has fewer than 100 employees.

Todd Who are your major competitors?

Judy Have you ever heard of this software company "McM"? It's one of the top 10 software companies.

Todd Sounds like you landed a good job.

Judy I know I shouldn't complain. I really lucked out this time.

Comprehension Questions
- Q1. How does Judy like her new job?
- Q2. What did Judy do before she got this job?
- Q3. What are good and bad points of Judy's job?
- Q4. What does the expression, "You can't have your cake and eat it, too," mean?

3. Language Practice

A Chunks & Chew
Complete the sentences with the appropriate words and expressions from the dialogue.

- ☐ landed / job
- ☐ bumped into
- ☐ pay hikes
- ☐ get / perks
- ☐ flexible hours

① The employees working for tech companies _____ the best _____ in the Boston area.
② She not only maintains _____ but also encourages everyone to follow her lead.
③ Guess who I _____ at the store last night?
④ I just _____ the best _____ in the world!
⑤ They received _____ of about 7% last year.

B Key Patterns
Here are some key patterns that you can use when talking about your company.

① How do you like _____ ?
- working with Johnson
- your new house
- the training course

② To be honest with you, _____ .
- I am a bit surprised at this article
- I've had a few problems recently
- I have nothing else to say at the moment

③ I'm responsible for _____ .
- managing customer relations at work
- supporting my family
- what I say

4. Role Plays

Read each situation and role play with your partner.

• 01 Situation

You are assigned to give a presentation on the new product line in front of potential customers who don't know much about your company and products. You are discussing what has to be prepared during a team meeting.

• 02 Situation

You are having a meeting with one of your major clients. During the meeting, the client asks you to evaluate your strengths in terms of how they compare to those of your competitors.

• 03 Situation

You just met a new employee at your company who has been working there for a few days. After introducing yourself, you want to make some polite small-talk and fill him/her in on the work culture and office environment.

5. Discussion

Discuss the following questions in detail.

1. Is it important that all members of your company know the proper way to make clients introductions?
2. What is the most effective way to promote your business/products or services?
3. How do you introduce yourself and your company to a new client?
4. What are some good tips to make a great first impression in business?
5. Would you rather have better perks or a higher salary?

Business Basics

Small Company vs. Large Company

There are some advantages in working for a small company and for a large company. Which type of company are you working for? Do you agree with the advantages that are listed below?

Working for a Small Company
- ☐ Getting attention is easy and your talent can be easily recognized.
- ☐ Climbing the ladder to a higher post can be faster as well.
- ☐ It is easy to know the whole organization.
- ☐ You will come to know about different departments' working conditions as well.
- ☐ Performing many tasks helps develop your entrepreneurial abilities.
- ☐ You work closely with high-level people.
- ☐ Less strict policies about working hours and days off.

Working for a Large Company
- ☐ They have lots of perks and better benefit packages.
- ☐ You have more opportunities to get systematic training courses.
- ☐ You will get the chance to specialize and more fully develop a specific expertise.
- ☐ You have more chances to meet various people.
- ☐ You enjoy stronger brand recognition or awareness.

One Point Lesson

Compare to vs. Compare with

✗ "The managers will visit our office and compare our plans to their own."

◎ "The managers will visit our office and compare our plans with their own."

"Compare to" describes someone or something as being similar to someone or something else. It is to point out or imply resemblances between objects. For example, you can say, "The teacher compared the child to a noisy monkey."

"Compare with" examines two or more people/things/ideas to discover similarities and/or differences.

6. Business Skills - Presentation Skills

In business meetings, usually the first meeting with the client involves a presentation to provide a detailed description or introduction to your company and the services it provides or the products it sells. Most presentations are divided into 3 main parts: introduction, body, and conclusion.

01 INTRODUCTION
- **Welcome your audience** (Greeting, your name, your position, your responsibilities)
- **Introduce your subject** (The title)
- **Outline the structure of your presentation** (How many parts, how many minutes, what you'll talk about)
- **Give instructions about questions** (Take questions during presentation or at the end)

02 BODY
- **Introducing the subject** (The purpose of your presentation)
- **Starting one subject** (First…)   • **Starting another** (Second…)
- **Analyzing a point** (Why it is important)   • **Giving an example** (To demonstrate…)

03 CONCLUSION
- **Sum up** (Conclusions)   • **Give recommendations if appropriate**
- **Thank your audience**   • **Invite questions**

[A] Categorizing — Following is a list of expressions used in the three parts of presentations. Write the number for each phrase in the correct section of that part of the presentation.

Introduction	Part 2 Body	Part 3 Conclusion
②,		

① Now, I'll summarize my presentation.
② Good morning, ladies and gentlemen. ✓
③ Second, I'll discuss what we do….
④ Do you have any questions?
⑤ My presentation will be in three parts: our company, our services, and the benefits….
⑥ Please wait until the end if you have any questions.
⑦ First, let me tell you about our company's history….
⑧ Thank you very much for your attention.
⑨ I would like to finish by saying…
⑩ My name is William Anderson. I am a senior manager in charge of sales and marketing.
⑪ Finally, I'll discuss the advantages to your company….
⑫ To demonstrate my point, here's an example….

[B] Presentation practice — **[Situation]** You are a sales representative for a furniture company, specifically tables. You have to give a presentation to a client about your company. Your company has been in business since 1980; you make tables from oak, maple, and cherry wood. You are the best company because you offer low prices even though you have the highest quality tables.

Work in pairs and use the following chart to organize your presentation:

- ☐ Greeting
- ☐ Self-introduction
- ☐ Title of presentation
- ☐ How many parts/how many minutes
- ☐ Questions until the end
- ☐ First (company history)
- ☐ Second (product description)
- ☐ Finally (benefit for client)
- ☐ Conclusion
- ☐ Recommendation
- ☐ Thank audience
- ☐ Ask for questions

Wrapping Up!

▶ 3 new words from this lesson

▶ 3 new expressions from this lesson

▶ 3 things to remember

Lesson 06
Work Environment

Learning Objectives

After completing this lesson, you will be able to...
- describe your working environment. (e.g., working hours, facilities)
- ask questions and talk about business life. (e.g., work and life balance)

OVERVIEW
☐ Warm Up Activities
☐ Useful Expressions
☐ Dialogue
☐ Language Practice
☐ Business Basics
☐ Role Plays
☐ Discussion
☐ One Point Lesson
☐ Business Skills

1. Warm Up Activities

A Discuss the following questions with a partner.

1. Would you prefer to work four ten-hour days or five eight-hour ones? Why?
2. What types of office equipment do you use on a daily basis? Is it convenient to use them?
3. How can you make your office cubicle feel more personal?

B Today's situation

Look at the situation and role play with your classmates.

> **"When You Try to Improve the Working Environment"**
>
> Nick is a supervisor in the HR Department. His team is involved in a new department planning project related to a healthy working environment. Nick's team members are having a meeting to set standards for establishing healthy work environments.
>
> **Nick:** A supervisor in the HR Department
> **Sarah and Greg:** Staff in the HR Department

Useful Expressions

A Talking about Work Environment

Match the expressions (1-5) with the similar meanings (a-e).

① Those are good points.
② What's your take on this?
③ Why don't we meet on Friday, the 13th?
④ We go hiking from time to time.
⑤ Can you go more in depth about it?

[ ] a. What are your thoughts about this?
[ ] b. Can you say a little bit more about it?
[ ] c. I can agree to your points.
[ ] d. We go hiking every now and then.
[ ] e. Are you free on Friday, the 13th?

B Degree of Certainty

Less Certain/Neutral	Very Certain
* I suppose so/not.	* Absolutely.
* I guess you're right.	* You're absolutely right.
* I might. I'm not sure.	* I totally agree with you.
* As far as I know, yes it is.	* I couldn't agree more.
* It probably will (won't).	* I'm sure it will (won't).

2. Dialogue

Read the dialogue and answer the questions with a partner.

Creating a Positive Working Environment

Nick We all know that a happy work environment results in harder workers. So, how can we create a trusted, productive, and positive work environment? Sarah, what's your take on this?

Sarah Well, the most important thing is to treat co-workers with the same respect you want to receive from them.

Nick Can you go more in depth about it? What are the best ways to demonstrate respect at work?

Sarah Well, for instance, we can listen to what others have to say before expressing our viewpoints. We should never talk over, butt in, or cut off another person.

Greg Right! Also, we shouldn't nitpick. People don't like being criticized over little things.

Nick Those are good points. Anything else?

Greg We can try making each and every cubicle a more welcoming place to work.

Sarah I totally agree with you. That way, it will seem less institutional when people swing by to visit from time to time.

Nick Yes. We work from 8:00 a.m. until 7:00 p.m. or later every day, which means we practically live here.

Sarah Why don't we mandate a clean desk policy? Each and every employee should clear and secure all paperwork and items by the end of the day.

Greg Oh, that sounds good. Then when you arrive in the morning, the tone is set for a peaceful day, right? That will work for me!

comprehension Questions
- Q1. What is the purpose of this meeting?
- Q2. What department do Sarah and Greg work in?
- Q3. What role does Nick play in this team meeting?
- Q4. What are some good points Sarah made during the meeting?

3. Language Practice

A Chunks & Chew

Complete the sentences with the appropriate words and expressions from the dialogue.

- ☐ talk over
- ☐ butting in
- ☐ swing by
- ☐ be set for
- ☐ in depth

① As soon as I win the lottery, I will _____ life!
② I told him we'd _____ his office about 5:00 today.
③ I haven't looked at the report _____ yet.
④ My boss is always _____ on our conversations.
⑤ As a child, I was taught that it's rude to interrupt and _____ someone else.

B Key Patterns

Here are some key patterns that you can use when talking about your working environment.

① **It seems**
_____.
- that you've decided already
- as if it is going to rain
- I can't seem to get through to you

② **What are the best ways**
_____?
- to quit smoking
- to motivate employees
- to maintain a true work-life balance

③ **Why don't we**
_____?
- meet after you're finished work
- focus on priority issues first
- go bowling tonight

Business Basics

Work Environment Factors

A positive work environment increases your work productivity and motivational level. The work environment should satisfy the physical and mental requirements of the people who work within it. What do you think is the most important factor? Why?

☐ **Positive Communication**
During a presentation or brainstorming session, avoid negative comments on ideas and be polite and calm during conflicts.

☐ **Trust**
Trust is a binding force between workers. Don't lie to co-workers, and don't get involved in gossip. Be helpful in the workplace.

☐ **Appreciation**
Appreciation is a key factor of a positive environment. This will improve the productivity and loyalty of the team members and also encourage others to achieve their goals.

☐ **Decorate Cubicle**
The physical working environment is an energizing factor. Some people put framed pictures of their loved ones or small plants on their desks.

4. Role Plays

Read each situation and role play with your partner.

You have worked in your current job for years. Your boss called you into his office to discuss performance evaluation. During the conversation, you want to request to change or set some office rules for a better workplace this time. Make some suggestions to your boss.

Your team just moved into another office which is too large for your team. Your team consists of only four members, and you do not want to work in a big, impersonal office. You want to add a little personality in your cubicle. Ask your colleagues for advice on making it a little more like home.

The CEO of your company is interested in starting monthly campaign, and this month's slogan is "Compliments to Co-workers." Your team members talk about how to compliment colleagues.

5. Discussion

Discuss the following questions in detail.

1. Based on your experience, what makes a good work environment?
2. What do you like or dislike most about your workplace?
3. Do you think workplace conversation improves the work-life balance? Why or why not?
4. Do people usually work for one company for a long time in your country, or is it common for people to change jobs every few years? Why do you think some people change jobs so often?
5. Have you ever experienced working in a hostile work environment? If so, what was your experience like? Based on your experience, what makes a good work environment?

By vs. Until — One Point Lesson

 We must make a decision until Tuesday.

 We must make a decision by Tuesday.

Both "until" and "by" indicate "any time before, but not later than." However, those two words are used differently. "Until" tells us how long a situation continues. If something happens until a particular time, you stop doing it at that time. For example, we can say "They lived in a small house until September."

"By" is often used to indicate a deadline. If something happens by a particular time, it happens at or before that time. For example, we can say, "We'd like to finish by August 31."

LESSON 06 / Work Environment 35

6. Business Skills - Describing Your Work Environment

The Human Resource Department is responsible for informing new employees about policies and what is required and expected in the workplace. However, because new employees want to make a good impression on their supervisors, they often feel shy about asking the boss or HR about specific requirements. They worry this might make them look like they are focused on their personal interests rather than on their job. They will usually ask co-workers for help in telling them about issues such as the facilities and working hours.

A Matching - Words that describe work hours and facilities

Match the words with the correct meanings.

1	office hours	A	Working without a company contract
2	day shift	B	Place where employees are allowed to smoke
3	cubicle	C	To work forty hours a week
4	freelance	D	Paid time off from work, usually one week
5	full time	E	Area where employees can eat or are allowed free time
6	vacation	F	To work/get paid for more than forty hours a week
7	sick pay	G	Employee work hours at night
8	night shift	H	Times the business is open
9	overtime	I	Small desk or area where employee works
10	smoking area	J	Employee works hours from 9 am to 5 pm
11	break room	K	Paid time off when employee is not well

B Discussing business and personal time balance

Fill in the blanks with words or phrases to describe the conversation.

Michael Hi. I haven't seen you before. You must be new here. I'm Michael, and you are…?

Andrew Oh hi, I'm Andrew. Nice to meet you, Michael. Actually, I usually work the ① _____. I'm never here before 5 pm. What about you – what shift do you usually work?

Michael Hey, nice to meet you, too. I always work the ② _____. There's no way I could work at night. I need to be home with my kids. Do you work forty hours a week? Are you ③ _____?

Andrew No, I actually ④ _____. I don't have a contract, but I do get to work as many hours as I want. I need to have a flexible schedule. I have young children. My wife works during the day. I work at night, so we can always have someone home with the kids.

Michael How do you like working here?

Andrew It's pretty good. I can work as much ⑤ _____ as I want. The extra money comes in handy. I still get ⑥ _____ if I have to miss work because the kids are sick. How about you?

Michael It's great! The ⑦ _____ are good, 9 am to 5 pm for me. Gives me a chance to spend time with my family and play a little golf on the weekends. They really have a great ⑧ _____ policy. I can take a week off every year and take the kids on trips.

Andrew I know what you mean. There are a lot of deadlines to meet in this job, so it's not always easy to make family time. Did you see the new ⑨ _____? They even put in a new cappuccino machine!

Michael I did! Do you smoke? They made a nice ⑩ _____ with tables and chairs up on the roof.

Andrew Sorry to say I do. But it is nice. I just wish my ⑪ _____ wasn't so small.

Michael Speaking of desks, I need to get back to mine. Nice talking to you. Hope I see you around.

Andrew Me, too. Take care!

Wrapping Up!

▶ 3 new words from this lesson

▶ 3 new expressions from this lesson

▶ 3 things to remember

Lesson 07
Following Company Policies

Learning Objectives
After completing this lesson, you will be able to...
- talk about your company's policies. (e.g., dress code, smoking, personal calls)
- exchange opinions on your company's policies.

OVERVIEW
- ☐ Warm Up Activities
- ☐ Useful Expressions
- ☐ Dialogue
- ☐ Language Practice
- ☐ Business Basics
- ☐ Role Plays
- ☐ Discussion
- ☐ One Point Lesson
- ☐ Business Skills
- ☐ Business Manner & Etiquette

1. Warm Up Activities

A Discuss the following questions with a partner.
1. What is the dress code where you work?
2. How often do you get a break (rest break, lunch break, etc.) at work?
3. What upsets you the most at work these days?

B Today's situation
Look at the situation and role play with your classmates.

"When Someone Breaks the Company Rules"

Jon broke the company rule by smoking inside the building. The team manager called Jon into his office and explained to him how important it is to follow the company policy. Jon promises not to break the rules again.

Useful Expressions

A Having a Conversation about Policy

Match the expressions (1-5) with the similar meanings (a-e).

① Do you have a minute to talk?
② I know everything is going to be fine.
③ I cannot come tomorrow as I have a prior engagement.
④ I will make sure it doesn't happen again.
⑤ You have a point.

- [ ] a. I am unable to attend the event because I will have to meet my clients tomorrow.
- [ ] b. I guarantee it isn't going to happen again.
- [ ] c. I see what you mean.
- [ ] d. I am well aware that things are going to be all right.
- [ ] e. Is this a good time to talk?

B Making Strong Recommendations
- **You should** (shouldn't) recruit any more staff.
- **I would advise** you to offer other languages.

C Suggesting Another Possibility
- **What (How) about** starting a training course?
- **Why don't you** e-mail some companies?

2. Dialogue
Read the dialogue and answer the questions with a partner.

Breaking Office Rules

Manager Jon, I need to talk to you about something. Do you have a minute to talk?

Jon Yes.

Manager Are you aware that smoking is prohibited in all of the enclosed areas within the worksites? One of the team members caught you smoking in the conference room. You know you are only allowed to smoke in the designated smoking area.

Jon Yes, I am aware of that, but it is unfair to smokers since we work on the 17th floor and the smoking area is all the way down on the first floor right next to the parking lot.

Manager Well, as you know, this company is committed to providing a healthy and safe environment for employees. Second-hand smoke is supposed to be worse for your health than smoking.

Jon You have a point. Also, I've been trying to quit smoking for quite some time. Thank you. Is there anything else you'd like to discuss before I get back to work? I am up to my neck in things to do. We are short-handed today because Mindy's been on a business trip since last week.

Manager Okay, just one more thing that's been bothering me lately. Smartphone usage during meetings. Just to let you know, I'm planning to restrict smartphone use in meetings.

Jon I see. I will make sure it won't happen again.

Manager Don't worry about it. Just remember for the future.

Comprehension Questions
- **Q1.** Why was Jon called into the manager's office?
- **Q2.** What rules does the company enforce for a healthy and safe environment?
- **Q3.** Why is Jon so busy at work this week?
- **Q4.** What has been annoying the manager during meetings?

3. Language Practice

A Chunks & Chew
Complete the sentences with the appropriate words and expressions from the dialogue.

- ☐ have a point
- ☐ break the rules
- ☐ get back to
- ☐ up to our necks
- ☐ short-handed

① Why is the boss talking about making cutbacks at a time when we're already _____?

② You _____. It would be better to wait until this evening.

③ You should not _____ at work to suit your own needs or interests.

④ We can't do anything more since we are already _____.

⑤ Can we _____ the point of this conversation?

B Key Patterns
Here are some key patterns that you can use when talking about your company policies.

① I'll make sure _____.
- we get the job done
- to maintain support and continue to improve
- to check that you haven't left anyone behind in the room

② I've been trying to _____.
- reach you all day long
- make this work for two months
- diet and work out

③ I'm supposed to _____.
- get my taxes back today
- finish my assignment by tomorrow
- get to work by 8:00 a.m

Business Basics
Setting Company Policies

More and more companies are setting employee gift policies. At a company in the United States, any gift worth more than $50 has to be reported. Some companies outright ban gifts of a certain value, but experts say that your company should be thinking about what dollar amount of a gift could potentially influence important business decisions. The following list presents other types of company policies. Which policies does your company have?

- ✓ Attendance and Punctuality
- ✓ Breaks, Lunch Times, Staff Lounge
- ✓ Computer Software
- ✓ Documents and Confidentiality
- ✓ Alcohol Use and Smoking Policy
- ✓ Harassment
- ✓ Office Dress Code
- ✓ Paychecks and Overtime Working
- ✓ Personal Phone Calls and Visitors

4. Role Plays

Read each situation and role play with your partner.

01 Situation You work in and are responsible for the summer internship training program. On the first day of the program, all the interns are invited to a local restaurant, and you are going to tell the new interns about your company policy.

02 Situation Your boss calls you into his office after he's seen you making personal calls a couple of times. He asks you if you are aware of the rules about personal phone calls at the office. He also asks if you have a reason to make those calls at work.

03 Situation Your team is having a team bonding dinner Friday night. At the dinner, your boss starts to talk about company and office rules and what could be inappropriate behavior in the workplace. Continue the conversation with your boss and share your opinions and thoughts.

5. Discussion

Discuss the following questions in detail.

1. Do you agree or disagree with the following statement? Standards of dress make a difference.
2. What are the rules of proper office etiquette including e-mail etiquette and cell phone etiquette?
3. Does your company have a written policy about workplace confidentiality guidelines? Discuss the importance of protecting confidential information with your partners.
4. Tell your partners about the ideal workplace environment and rules you would like to work in.
5. What kind of work rules does everyone easily break? Why?

Promise vs. Appointment

 A: Why don't you have lunch with me today?
B: I would love to, but I have a promise.

◎ A: Why don't you have lunch with me today?
B: I would love to, but I have an appointment.

One Point Lesson

Some people confuse these two words because both of them are related to "something announced to do in the future." However, the two are used differently in different situations. "Promise" is a commitment by someone to do or not to do something. It is a commitment which you make to a person that you will definitely do something. "Appointment" is an arrangement to do something or to meet someone at a particular time and space. If you have an appointment with someone, you arrange to see him/her in advance at a particular time.

6. Business Skills - Dress for Success

What's appropriate to wear to work? In many companies, there are no <u>set-in-stone rules</u>, so when in doubt, go traditional. "The most basic mistake new employees make is <u>underdressing</u>," says Randall Hansen, a professor of business at Stetson University in Deland, Florida. "If unsure, dress conservatively. The best way to avoid a problem is to understand the <u>corporate culture</u>." That's a polite way of saying that a <u>button-down</u> company won't appreciate your showing up for work in cutoffs and flip-flops.

Making the right impression at work isn't hard if you keep in mind three basic points when buying clothes for the office:

1. Presentation counts.
2. Casual shouldn't mean <u>slovenly</u>.
3. Dress as you want to be seen: serious, professional, <u>upward-bound</u>, and ready to meet clients.

For men, traditional attire includes:
- A button-down shirt.
- Polished black shoes.
- A blue, black, or gray jacket.
- Slacks that complement the jacket.
- You can't go wrong with a conservative tie.

For women, the traditional look includes:
- A skirt that hits just above the knee, slacks, or perhaps a pantsuit.
- Simple jewelry.
- Just a hint of makeup. Skip the perfume.
- Sweaters.
- Pantyhose may be the office standard.

(1) Discuss the difference between casual clothes and formal clothes. Why does it make a difference? Why is it important?

....

....

(2) Work in pairs to rewrite informal expressions into formal terms.

[Examples]

Informal	Formal
Listen up	Listen carefully to this very important information

[Practice]

Carved in stone	inflexible	Button-down	
Underdressing		Slovenly	
Corporate culture		Upward-bound	

Business Manner & Etiquette
Benefits of Establishing a Dress Code in the Workplace

Appropriate dress, along with basic etiquette, is one of the most common associations made to professionalism. We form first impressions and overall judgments about people by the way they dress.

"Each employee is expected to present a neat, well-groomed and business-like appearance reasonably attuned to contemporary moods and attitudes. Extreme fashions are not considered appropriate business attire and are discouraged."

"Employee apparel appropriateness will be determined by the immediate supervisor. Supervisors may take into consideration whether there is direct contact with the public sector and the work area."

"Professional appearance will vary. Impeccable personal hygiene is the beginning of acceptable professional appearance. Shoes should be clean and neat with appropriate heel according to the work environment."

Wrapping Up!

▶ 3 new words from this lesson

▶ 3 new expressions from this lesson

▶ 3 things to remember

Lesson 08
Prospecting the Future

Learning Objective

After completing this lesson, you will be able to...
- ask and answer questions about new products and their brands on the market.
- compare different aspects of companies and assess your company's value.

OVERVIEW
☐ Warm Up Activities
☐ Useful Expressions
☐ Dialogue
☐ Language Practice
☐ Business Basics
☐ Role Plays
☐ Discussion
☐ One Point Lesson
☐ Business Skills

1. Warm Up Activities

A Discuss the following questions with a partner.
1. Is your company planning to launch a new product? Who is your target market?
2. Who are your company's major competitors?
3. How does your company differentiate itself from its competitors?

B Today's situation
Look at the situation and role play with your classmates.

"When You Describe Company Values"

David Miller is heading to Frankfurt on business. David finds an empty seat on the plane and introduces himself and his business to Ken Burns, the person who is sitting beside him.

David Miller: Works for a mobile communication service provider
Ken Burns: Works for a Frankfurt-based global company

Useful Expressions

A Describing Products

- This is the newly launched product.
- It has several special features.
- One of the most useful features is its energy-saving design.
- It is made of wood and steel.
- It comes in a wide range of colors

B Talking about Company & Market

Match the expressions (1-5) with the similar meanings (a-e).

① Are you heading for Tokyo?
② We launched our new website.
③ We've finalized the details for the event.
④ Their reputation has been called into question.
⑤ The housing market rebounded last month.

☐ a. The real estate market has finally made the turn to recovery.
☐ b. Are you traveling to Tokyo?
☐ c. We introduced a new look for our website.
☐ d. Growing risks to their profitability raised doubts about their reputation.
☐ e. We finally settled on the details for the event.

2. Dialogue

Read the dialogue and answer the questions with a partner.

Describing Company Values

David Excuse me. Is this seat taken?
Ken No, it isn't. Please have a seat.
David Thanks. David Miller. Pleased to meet you.
Ken Ken Burns. Are you heading for Frankfurt?
David Yes, I have some business there. I work for a mobile communication service provider, EU-Mobile.
Ken EU-Mobile? Isn't that the company that launched the first generation analog in Europe?
David Yes. In fact, that is one of the reasons I am flying to Germany. We've just launched EUTouch 4G, one of the largest touch screens offered by any of the major carriers.
Ken Oh, I read an article on that this morning. I also read about how your company's stock prices suffered last year and that the value of the stock has also been called into question.
David True, it was very discouraging, but we really pulled ourselves together and got over the hump! The stock prices rebounded soon after launching EUTouch 4G.
Ken Yes, I've noticed that, too.
David How about you? What brings you to Frankfurt?
Ken I have some business there as well. To be honest, I work for a global trading company in Frankfurt.

Comprehension Questions

Q1. Where does this conversation take place?
Q2. What is the purpose of David's visit to Germany?
Q3. What kind of company does David work for?

3. Language Practice

A Chunks & Chew

Complete the sentences with the appropriate words and expressions from the dialogue.

- ☐ work on
- ☐ called into question
- ☐ bring / to
- ☐ pulled together
- ☐ get over the hump

① She will _____ her colleagues _____ the conference.
② Everyone on our street really _____ after the storm.
③ He will have to _____ getting fit before the game.
④ When you _____, life is much better.
⑤ I'm not used to having my abilities _____.

B Key Patterns

Here are some key patterns that you can use when talking about your company's value.

① That is one of the reasons _____.
- we crave chocolate sometimes
- men love going out for a drink after work
- my team always comes up with a good performance

② _____ soon after _____.
- I got a decent job / graduation
- It is unacceptable to leave a job / you started
- The material should be distributed to the participants / the meeting

③ _____ (be) heading to/for _____.
- I (am) / the pub for a beer after work
- I (was) / the coast when you called me last night
- We (are) / the movies after we finished the class

Business Basics

Ways to Promote Sales

In marketing, a promotion is the sum of all activities undertaken to improve sales. Here are some ideas on how to promote sales and your business.

Targeted to Customers	Targeted to Company Salespeople, Intermediaries, and their Sales Forces
☐ Coupon (incl. online issue) ☐ Cents-off Offers ☐ Free Samples ☐ Cash Rebates (money-refund offers) ☐ Premiums ☐ Consumer Contest ☐ Sweepstakes ☐ Consumer Exhibitions	☐ Sales Meetings ☐ Sales Contests ☐ Point-of-purchase Display ☐ Trade Shows ☐ Store Demonstration ☐ Dealer Salespeople Incentives ☐ Annual Partnership Advantage ☐ Additional Project Deals

4. Role Plays

Read each situation and role play with your partner.

• 01 Situation

You are an office worker in Shanghai. Your manager is asking you to give a presentation to potential investors. Your team is running a brainstorming meeting to help you prepare your presentation. Talk to your partners and make suggestions on a detailed outline of the presentation.

• 02 Situation

You work in the marketing division. Your team members have been discussing your new marketing strategy after launching a new product. Your team leader asks you to identify your business's target market to best serve and advertise directly to your target customers.

• 03 Situation

You are a PR manager in the United States. A reporter called today to interview you about how to maintain a good company image. Give the reporter some tips on how to keep a company's professional image.

5. Discussion

Discuss the following questions in detail.

1. What are your company's strengths and weaknesses versus its major competitors?
2. How is your company performing in respect to sales and profits?
3. What is your company's business strategy? What are the key objectives for your company over the next one to five years?
4. Who are your company's major or target customers? What is your niche?
5. How satisfied are your customers with your company's performance in meeting their needs or expectations?

One Point Lesson

Economic vs. Economical

 They want people to buy more economic cars.

 They want people to buy more economical cars.

"Economic" and "economical" are frequently used interchangeably, but strictly speaking they have quite distinct meanings. "Economical" is used to describe methods, products, machines, etc. that are not expensive or do not waste money or other resources. However, the word "economic" is used to describe things that are related to the economy of a country and how well it is performing.

6. Business Skills - Questions about New Products

Businesses need to do brand research when developing a new product. This is a general list of words used among target customers. This gives companies significant opportunities to better understand customers and what motivates them. They can adjust their marketing messages for their customers. This strengthens their brand in the minds of customers.

 Vocabulary used to describe brands

Categorize the following words to fit the appropriate meaning. Then, talk about the meanings.

- disadvantage
- merits
- characteristics
- hindrance
- superior
- value
- properties
- impediment
- hitch
- obstacle
- status
- defect
- choice
- attributes
- faults
- hurdle
- exceptional
- excellent
- select
- features
- wrinkle
- flaw
- quality
- shortcomings
- downfall
- worth
- barrier

Positive

Neutral

Negative

02 Discussing brands and comparisons

Work in pairs using the following questions to discuss **Apple's iPhone**. Use the vocabulary above to discuss the Apple iPhone's qualities, drawbacks, and features as well as its competitors. You can replace "**this brand**" with the product name. Next, discuss in pairs what other "hot" brands or products are bestsellers. Who is their competition in today's market?

* Apple's iPhone
*
*
*

① When you think of **this brand**, what are the first words that come to mind?
② When and why did you first become a customer of **this brand**?
③ Why do you continue to be a customer of **this brand**?
④ Who do you consider to be competitors of **this brand**?
⑤ How is **this brand** different from its competitors (in terms of being both better and worse)?
⑥ How is **this brand** the same as its competitors?
⑦ How can the customer experience of **this brand** be improved?
⑧ Do you anticipate that you will be a customer of **this brand** in the future?
⑨ If you were describing **this brand** to others, what would you say, and would you recommend it?

Wrapping Up!

▶ 3 new words from this lesson

▶ 3 new expressions from this lesson

▶ 3 things to remember

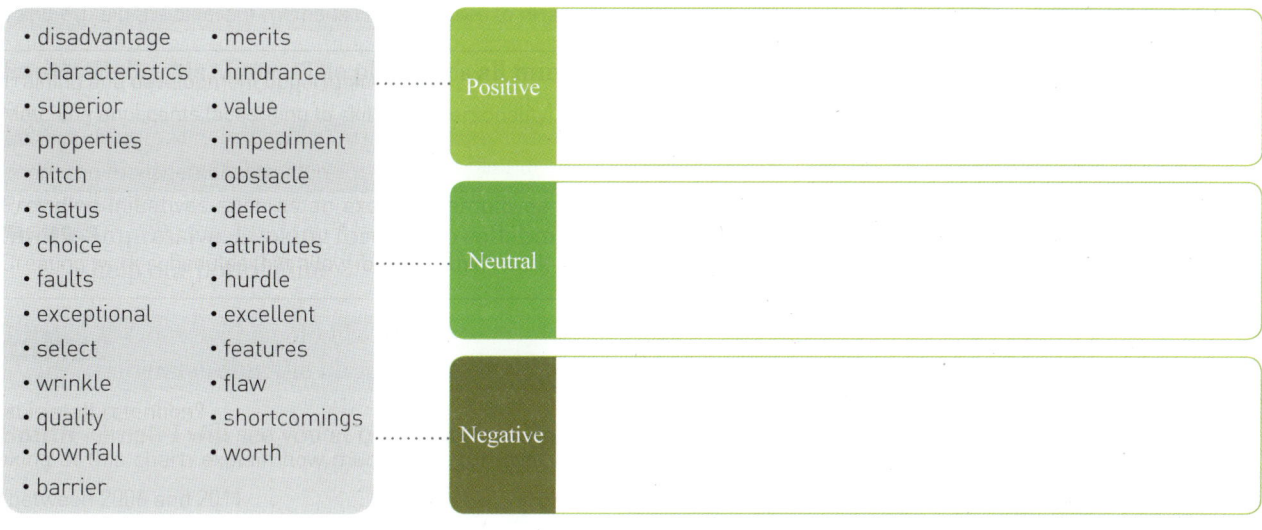

02 Focus on Sustainability

Business Practice 1

Balfour Beatty Construction

◉ Background

Balfour Beatty Construction is an international commercial construction company, headquartered in Dallas, Texas, with full service offices in the United States. In over 80 countries, the company operates a wide-ranging portfolio with client sectors including healthcare, K-12 education, and military housing.

During the first half of the year, the company was encouraged by the improvement in the leading indicators and its new work in the US. However, this has not led to a consistent positive trend in the institutional building market. The reduction caused a drop in profits from £15 billion down to £14.4 billion. £500 million is in construction; three-quarters of that is within the US, and one-quarter of that is within the UK. The construction order book for 2013 was down 20% versus the same level last year. The business is continuing to migrate toward smaller contracts in a market with very few major projects.

◉ Breakthrough Thinking

Read the following and answer the questions.

> Looking at 2013-2015, Balfour Beatty expects to have limited visibility due to smaller projects and shorter lead times. The assumption is that market conditions will not improve, and they expect a further decline in activity levels and pressure on margins.

Q1) What do you think are the major reasons for the decreased amount of construction?

....

e.g., difficult market conditions, lower volumes & loss of competitive pricing, supply chain suffering, etc.

Q2) What do you think can be the breakthrough for Balfour Beatty Construction?

....

◉ Sustainability

They plan to make progress by restructuring operations. One of proposed ideas is to focus on "sustainability." Here's an excerpt from recent company literature distributed to clients and employees:

> "Going green isn't just the latest fad, but a very necessary part of evolving and leading the growth of our industry."

This new Roadmap sets out the exciting next stage of our sustainability journey, laying out the milestones for 2015. The Roadmap articulates the strategies necessary to ensure the long-term viability of Balfour Beatty. These include strategies that address the challenges of sustainable development that face the world as a whole, including the followings.

- ✓ Deforestation
- ✓ Climate change
- ✓ Energy demand
- ✓ Conflict
- ✓ Urbanization
- ✓ Poverty
- ✓ Transport growth
- ✓ Biodiversity

CASE STUDY 02

[Example] Balfour Beatty Rail is developing new technologies for the Italian rail industry through a partnership with the Polytechnic of Milan and railway infrastructure manager "Rete Ferroviaria Italiana" (RFI). RFI are looking to integrate alternatives to overhead copper contact wire which can pose threats to the environment. Copper particles can accumulate in and near the railway resulting in potential ground contamination. Copper is also a relatively rare commodity. Balfour Beatty Rail is assessing two alternative design solutions to the traditional all-copper approach: one all-aluminium and one a copper-aluminium mix. Benefits of the solution for RFI will be lower costs in installation and maintenance and a more sustainable approach.

◎ Analyze

01 Discuss the following:
- What does sustainability mean?
- Why is it important?
- How is sustainability accomplished?
- Who benefits from it?

02 Refer to the following table to discuss why sustainability is important to the company.

☐ Brand Enhancement	Improves how customers, regulators, investors, communities and the value chain feel about your organization and its products or services.
☐ Innovation Driver	Create products and services for a burgeoning market that cares about "green"; reduce the environmental footprint of production process, waste stream and product.
☐ Risk Mitigation	Reduction and elimination of hazardous or toxic materials in supply chain reduces regulatory exposure and risk of worker or customer health impacts.
☐ Asset Value Enhancement	Green companies showing premium valuations; green buildings showing improved lease and sale value, lower vacancy.
☐ Market Opportunity	Increasingly, public agencies and institutional investment funds require a sustainability filter for their investments as well as product and vendor selections.
☐ Cost Savings	Reduced cost of energy, water, waste disposal, and savings on material inputs.
☐ Workforce Engagement	Attract, motivate and retain top personnel in a competitive talent market.

◎ Presentation

Your client plans to build a hotel in a city. He feels sustainability is too expensive and will increase the construction costs. In addition, it will limit his profits because he will not be able to pass on the extra construction costs to the occupants of his buildings. Prepare and deliver a presentation detailing how this will benefit him and his business.

Bullet Points of Your Presentation

* ....
* ....
* ....

Lesson 09
Leaving a Message

Learning Objectives
After completing this lesson, you will be able to...
- talk on the phone and take or leave a message.
- use appropriate telephone etiquette.

OVERVIEW
☐ Warm Up Activities
☐ Useful Expressions
☐ Dialogue
☐ Language Practice
☐ Business Basics
☐ Role Plays
☐ Discussion
☐ One Point Lesson
☐ Business Skills

1. Warm Up Activities

A Discuss the following questions with a partner.
1. How much time do you spend every day on your phone?
2. Do your team members have good telephone manners when they take messages?
3. Do you prefer calling or texting for communication?

B Today's situation
Look at the situation and role play with your classmates.

"He is not available right now."

Rich asked Jack to make his business cards by today. Now Jack calls Rich to ask him to stop by and pick up his business cards; however, Rich is not in the office at the moment. Lisa, the receptionist, takes a message for Jack.

Jack: An employee at Kentlaw Printers Inc., in charge of making business cards.
Lisa: Rich's receptionist, who ordered business cards from Jack

Useful Expressions

A Asking for Connection and Responding

Asking to be transferred
* I'd like to speak to (a name).
* Could/Can/May I speak to (a name)?
* Could you put me through to (a name)?

Being unavailable
* I'm afraid he/she is in a meeting.
* He is not in the office.
* He is still at lunch.

B Talking on the Telephone

Match the expressions (1-4) with the similar meanings (a-d).

① I'm afraid he's on the other line.
② Can you put me through to Jennifer Kim?
③ I better give my phone number to you, just to be sure.
④ He's not at his desk at the moment.

☐ a. Could you transfer me to extension 42?
☐ b. I'm sorry, but he can't take your call right now.
☐ c. I'll give it to you just in case she doesn't have my number.
☐ d. He is not in the office right now.

2. Dialogue

Read the dialogue and answer the questions with a partner.

Not Available Right Now

Lisa Good Afternoon. ZZZ Corporation. How may I assist you?

Jack Hello. Can you put me through to Rich Remy, please?

Lisa I'm sorry. He's not at his desk at the moment.

Jack Do you know when he'll be back?

Lisa He should be back by 1:00. Would you like to leave a message for him?

Jack Yes. Do you have a pen handy?

Lisa Hold on a moment. Okay, go ahead.

Jack Could you tell him the business cards are ready for pick-up? To my knowledge, he wanted us to get it done by this afternoon.

Lisa Certainly. Can I have your name, please?

Jack My name is Jack Orsillo. I'm with Kentlaw Printers. Also, could you have him call me when he has a spare moment? I need to discuss the billing details.

Lisa Does he have your number?

Jack I think so, but I better give it to you, just to be sure. It's 801-226-2422.

Lisa All right, Mr. Orsillo. I'll have him call you when he gets back in the office.

Jack Thanks. I appreciate it. Have a nice day.

Comprehension Questions

- **Q1.** What is the name of the caller?
- **Q2.** According to Lisa, what is Rich doing at the moment?
- **Q3.** Why is Jack calling Rich?
- **Q4.** Where does Jack work?

3. Language Practice

A. Chunks & Chew

Complete the sentences with the appropriate words and expressions from the dialogue.

- ☐ put me through
- ☐ to my knowledge
- ☐ (be) not handy
- ☐ get a spare moment
- ☐ picks up

① _____, the company hasn't taken a position on that precisely.

② The lady always _____ and drops off the laundry on time.

③ Will you please _____ to the international operator?

④ I do it whenever I _____.

⑤ I am _____ when it comes to fixing things – around the house or in general.

B. Key Patterns

Here are some key patterns that you can use when talking on the phone.

① _____ get/have _____ + *past participle*.
- I / my car / (wash) at that new place by the station
- We / a pizza / (deliver) yesterday
- I will / my coats / (clean) soon

② I appreciate _____. / I'd appreciate it if _____.
- your honesty/your support/your patience
- your taking the time to review my report
- you could tell me what time you can come

③ _____, just to be sure.
- Maybe you should double-check
- I will try all the wrong ones before
- I always proofread my own work

Business Basics

Telephone Etiquette

Here are some basic guidelines for proper usage of the telephone. Place check marks beside the five you think are the most important points of etiquette.

- [ ] Identify yourself immediately to the other person.
- [ ] Focus yourself clearly on the purpose of the call and the person with whom you are speaking.
- [ ] E-mail ahead if you want to make sure the other person has time to prepare for the call.
- [ ] Place your call during normal business hours.
- [ ] When leaving a message for someone you have called, speak slowly and clearly.
- [ ] Don't rely on your memory: make notes during a call and rewrite them if possible.
- [ ] All incoming calls should be answered in a timely manner.
- [ ] When you call someone, ask if they have a moment to speak with you.
- [ ] If you get the wrong number, apologize to the person who answers the phone.
- [ ] Send a follow-up e-mail to confirm any important details and have a written record.

4. Role Plays

Read each situation and role play with your partner.

01 You work in an office and receive a telephone call for your co-worker, Bill Johnson. Bill is currently out of the office. Take a message and make sure you get the following information:
- Name and telephone number
- Ask the person to spell his/her family name
- Message he/she would like to leave for Bill
- How late Bill can call him/her at the given phone number

02 You purchased your laptop online and just received it yesterday. This morning, you find out that the laptop screen keeps turning black but not off. Call and leave a message to a customer service representative to file a complaint.

03 You need to purchase two new copy machines for your office. Call Black & White Copiers and ask for the following information:
- Any special offers   - Warranty   - Discounted pricing   - The location of the nearest repair center

5. Discussion

Discuss the following questions in detail.

1. How do you communicate with foreign partners who are in another place/country?
2. How do you feel when you have to communicate in English on the phone with someone who doesn't speak English very well?
3. What is the proper telephone etiquette for business, especially when leaving messages?
4. When leaving voicemails for clients/customers, what information do you include with the message?
5. Describe an experience when you had a hard time leaving a message in a foreign language.

One Point Lesson

Hear vs. Listen to

❌ He heard carefully every word I said.

⭕ He listened carefully to every word I said

"Listen to" is "to hear and pay attention to." It is used to talk about or describe sounds that are being made around you and which you are making an active effort to focus on.

In contrast, to "hear" something happens without any intentional effort. You can hear something even when you don't want to hear it and don't try to hear it. For example, you could say, "She heard a noise outside."

6. Business Skills - Talking on the Phone

Making business calls is sometimes necessary and very important for many reasons, such as to schedule business meetings, confirm information, make arrangements for visitors, or change plans. You should make sure the information needed is clear as well as polite.

A Leaving a message

Fill in the blanks with the following expressions to describe the conversation.

[Situation]
Angela is giving a presentation next week to IBM. She is going out of town all week and won't be available by e-mail, so she's calling Robert to confirm the time of the meeting before she leaves.

[Expressions]

a) Is he available?
b) Would you like to leave a message?
c) What can I do for you today?
d) Will do.
e) What have you been up to?
f) I'm afraid he is not at his desk.
g) Looking forward to it.
h) Can I put you on hold and I'll see if he's in?
i) Are you staying busy?

Betty: Good morning, IBM. How may I help you?
Angela: Good morning, Betty, this is Angela. How are you today?
Betty: Oh hi, Angela. I'm pretty good. How about you?
(1)_____?
Angela: Nothing much, just working.
(2)_____?
Betty: Yes, I am! You know how it is.
(3)_____?
Angela: Well, I was calling to speak to Robert.
(4)_____?
Betty: (5)_____?
Angela: Sure. Thanks.

Betty: Angela, (6)_____.
(7)_____?
Angela: Yes, can you please tell him I'm going out of town and won't be available by e-mail? I need to confirm the time of next week's meeting. I'll be in my office until 2 p.m. Please have him call me ASAP.
Betty: (8)_____.
Angela: Thanks, Betty! See you next week.
Betty: (9)_____.
Take care.
Angela: You, too. Bye!
Betty: Bye!

B Telephone role play

Work in pairs to practice dialogue.

[Situation]
Casey is calling Mr. Carter, the manager of BMW, to schedule a lunch meeting at the restaurant Key West. Mr. Carter isn't in, and Maggie is answering the phones. Casey needs to leave a message, but Maggie doesn't understand Casey when he says the name of the restaurant.

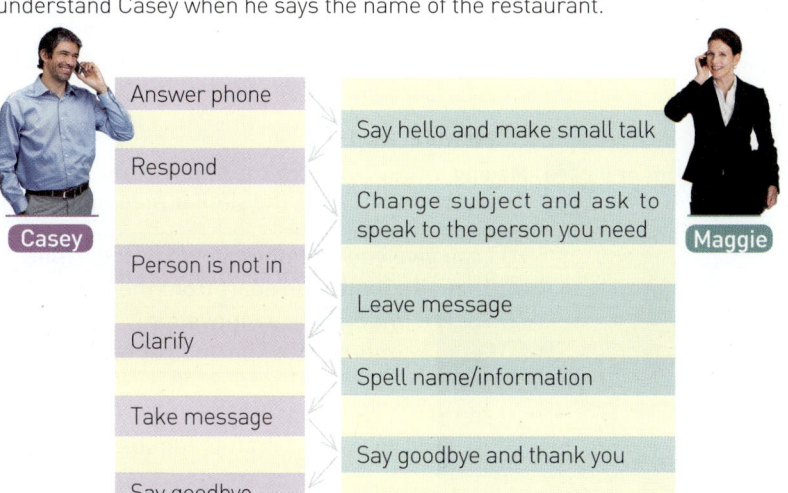

Wrapping Up!

▶ 3 new words from this lesson

▶ 3 new expressions from this lesson

▶ 3 things to remember

Lesson 10
Making Arrangements

Learning Objectives
After completing this lesson, you will be able to...
- make arrangements with other people.
- select an ideal time and a place for a global meeting.

OVERVIEW
☐ Warm Up Activities
☐ Useful Expressions
☐ Dialogue
☐ Language Practice
☐ Business Basics
☐ Role Plays
☐ Discussion
☐ One Point Lesson
☐ Business Skills

1. Warm Up Activities

A Discuss the following questions with a partner.

1. Was it easy for you to pick the best time for a meeting or for a conference call with participants around globe?
2. Have you ever had to make arrangements for a place to hold a meeting? What was the meeting for?
3. Have you ever booked a venue for a conference? If yes, when was it?

B Today's situation
Look at the situation and role play with your classmates.

"When you should make an arrangement"

Sean calls the conference venue to book a conference room. The staff member takes down all the information Sean gives during the phone conversation. They are undergoing a renovation, so it won't be open in the middle of December. Sean will call the staff again after discussing the date change with his boss.

Useful Expressions

A	Asking about Availability	- When would be a convenient time to meet? - When are you free? (less formal)
B	Suggesting Dates/Time/Places	- Would 8:30 be okay? - Would Tuesday suit you? - Would you be available on Tuesday? - How does Friday after dinner sound? - How about if we meet Friday evening?
C	Accepting and Refusing	- I'm afraid I can't make it then. - That suits me fine. / It is fine with me. - I'm sorry; I've got something else going on.

D Making Arrangements — Match the expressions (1-4) with the similar meanings (a-d).

① I can give you a brief rundown of the event.
② That all sounds fine apart from the date.
③ We are undergoing a renovation.
④ Let me confirm with him and get back to you.

[ ] a. The building is currently under renovation.
[ ] b. I will call you back after I double-check with him.
[ ] c. I can fill you in with a quick summary of the event.
[ ] d. Everything sounds good except for the date.

2. Dialogue
Read the dialogue and answer the questions with a partner.

Locating a Venue for a Conference

Sean Hi, I would like to inquire about your venue for a conference I am arranging for my company.

Staff Sure, thank you for calling. Can you provide me with some details about the event? I'll find out what's possible for you.

Sean Actually, I don't have all the details at the moment. If it is okay with you, I can give you a brief rundown of the event.

Staff Sure, not a problem. Go ahead.

Sean The conference should take place on a weekday in the middle of December. It will be a full-day program attended by around 200 people, and we will require lunch and dinner as well as refreshments for the duration of the event.

Staff Okay. That all sounds fine apart from the date. We are undergoing a renovation until the middle of December. Would you be able to push it back to the last week of the month?

Sean That shouldn't be a problem, but let me confirm with my VP and get back to you.

Staff Sure thing.

Comprehension Questions
Q1. What is the purpose of this phone conversation?
Q2. What is Sean looking for, exactly?
Q3. When does Sean need a conference room, and for what?
Q4. Why isn't the conference venue available in the middle of December?

3. Language Practice

A Chunks & Chew
Complete the sentences with the appropriate words and expressions from the dialogue.

- ☐ confirm / with
- ☐ give / a rundown
- ☐ take place
- ☐ push / back to
- ☐ apart from

① Can I .... our meeting .... sometime next month?
② Oh sorry, the meeting will .... at Room 345, not 435.
③ .... the ending, it's a really good film.
④ Please .... your participation .... my secretary by this Friday.
⑤ Make sure to .... your boss .... on what he missed while he was away.

B Key Patterns
Here are some key patterns that you can use when making arrangements.

① _____ provide _____ with _____ .
- This conference must / your sales team / inspiration
- This meeting / me / the opportunity to offer assistance
- We / them / money and clothes

② Would _____ be able to _____ ?
- you / send it by e-mail today
- he / help me put it together
- they / produce additional documents

③ _____ get back to _____ .
- I will / you on that
- I can / you on those figures by the end of the day
- He is still struggling to / his normal life

Business Basics

What Would You Do in these Situations?

1. You have an appointment at a client's office at 11:00 a.m. What time would you arrive?
2. A client asks you to phone her at 3:00 p.m. at her office. What time would you call?
3. A business meeting starts at 10:00 a.m. What time would you arrive?
4. A client asks you to call him at his home, but not later than 11:00 p.m. What time would you call?
5. You arrange to meet a client at a hotel bar at 7:30 p.m. He doesn't arrive or answer your call.
   You call his office, but there is no reply. What time would you leave the bar?
6. You are invited to a party at a colleague's house at 8:00 p.m. What time would you arrive?
7. You are halfway through a meeting and a participant arrives late. What do you say?

4. Role Plays

Read each situation and role play with your partner.

01 Situation

You want to make an appointment with Ms. Johnson to discuss a possible business partnership. However, Ms. Johnson is unavailable, and you are transferred to her voice mail. Leave a voicemail message for her. Your phone number is 422-2757.

02 Situation

Your boss just told you that he won't be able to go to the client's meeting tonight. You arranged the meeting with the client two weeks ago. Call the client and explain to him/her why your boss can't make it to the meeting tonight.

03 Situation

On your way to an important lunch meeting, you are rear-ended in a car accident. Call your client, who is waiting for you at the meeting venue, and make a couple of suggestions for rescheduling.

5. Discussion

Discuss the following questions in detail.

1. What do you think the most important thing is when you are arranging a global meeting?
2. What is your experience with arranging a video conference? Do you prefer personal meetings or video conferences?
3. Discuss some pros and cons of video conferencing.
4. When was the last time you had to arrange a meeting/conference for your global teams?
5. Have you ever been involved in an accident on your way to a meeting? Were you able to make it to the meeting on time? If not, how did you make up for it?

One Point Lesson

Sensible vs. Sensitive

 "Steve takes his work seriously and is sensible to criticism."

 "Steve takes his work seriously and is sensitive to criticism."

"Sensible" means "reasonable and practical." We use the word to describe someone who makes good decisions based on reason and who never behaves in a stupid or dangerous way. We can say, "It would be sensible to consult everybody first."

We use "sensitive" to describe someone who is easily upset or offended: "She is very sensitive about her weight, so try not to mention it."

LESSON 10 / Making Arrangements

6. Business Skills - Scheduling a Meeting

In business, plans often need to be changed. People are often out of the office, in meetings, or not at their desks to be able to check their e-mail. Also, it's often necessary to make different arrangements. See the following phrases that are used to politely but clearly make arrangements or make plans.

Useful Phrases

Scheduling a meeting, responses:
01. No, I'm afraid Monday's out. What about Friday?
02. 1 o'clock at my office. That works for me.
03. Tuesday at 10 is best for me. Is that good for you?
04. How about 2 o'clock on Friday? What do you think?
05. 3:30 is good. Does that work for you?
06. Next week sounds good, say Tuesday at 3? What do you think?

Changing an appointment:
07. I'm sorry, but something has come up. Can we reschedule?
08. Is it possible to reschedule?
09. I'm so sorry this is last minute, but something has just crossed my desk, and I'm afraid I can't make it. Would you mind if we reschedule?
10. I've had a last-minute change here at the office, something that needs my full attention. Can we reschedule, please?

Being late:
11. My meeting is running over, I'll be about _____ minutes late. So sorry for the inconvenience.
12. Things are really hectic in the office; I could be a few minutes late. I hope that's okay.
13. I'm so sorry, but I'm running a little late.
14. So sorry, but traffic is crazy today. I'll be there ASAP.
15. I should be there by_____ at the latest. Thanks for your patience.
16. If I run into a snag that makes me late, I'll call you ASAP.

A)) Scheduling a meeting

What's the proper response for each sentence?

1. When do you think a good time would be for me to come by?
....
2. How about next week?
....
3. What's a good time for you next week?
....
4. Let's say 1 o'clock at your office?
....
5. Does Monday work for you?
....
6. What day works best for you?
....

B)) Coming to an agreement about meeting times

Look at the situation and role play.

[Situation]
Arthur has called Jeff at Delta Airlines to schedule a meeting to give a presentation. Linda, the receptionist, is answering the phone. Arthur has called Delta many times. Linda and Arthur have spoken many times, and by now, she knows him very well. She tried to put the call through to Jeff, but he is unavailable. Arthur wants to meet on Tuesday at 3, but Jeff can't meet then. Linda says he can meet on Friday at 10, and Arthur agrees.

Wrapping Up!

▶ 3 new words from this lesson

▶ 3 new expressions from this lesson

▶ 3 things to remember

Lesson 11
Exchanging Opinions

Learning Objectives
After completing this lesson, you will be able to...
- express your opinions effectively and make suggestions.
- brainstorm various ideas and mildly disagree with assertions from other participants.

OVERVIEW
☐ Warm Up Activities
☐ Useful Expressions
☐ Dialogue
☐ Language Practice
☐ Business Basics
☐ Role Plays
☐ Discussion
☐ One Point Lesson
☐ Business Skills

1. Warm Up Activities

A Discuss the following questions with a partner.

1. Have you ever run a brainstorming meeting?
2. How often do you have meetings?
3. Do you usually express your opinions actively when having business meetings?

B Today's situation

Look at the situation and role play with your classmates.

"When you have a brainstorming meeting"

Brian, the CEO of ABC Company, called a brainstorming meeting for fundraising ideas. Lucy, Don, and Stan participate in the meeting. They decide to discuss the matter further to hammer out a final solution.

Useful Expressions

A When You Have a Meeting

Match the expressions (1-5) with the similar meanings (a-e).

① We are in danger of closing.
② That sounds promising!
③ I think we're shooting too high.
④ We're out of time.
⑤ How does this idea sound?

____ a. That will work out really well.
____ b. It seems we are running short of time.
____ c. The plan exceeds its aim.
____ d. What's your take on this idea?
____ e. We are going out of business.

B Keeping a Meeting on Time

- Please be brief.
- Let's get back on track.
- I'm afraid that is outside the scope of this meeting.
- Keep to the point, please.
- I think we'd better leave that for another meeting.

2. Dialogue

Read the dialogue and answer the questions with a partner.

Running a Brainstorming Meeting

Brian I've called this meeting to brainstorm some fundraising ideas. As you know, we're in danger of closing. Any thoughts?

Lucy I thought that Jon was working on getting donors.

Brian He is, but we can't count on that coming through.

Don How much do we need to raise? What's a ballpark figure?

Brian We need at least $100,000 for the following fiscal year.

Don That's a lot of money, but I think we'll come up with something. How does a benefit performance sound?

Stan Oh, so all the takings can go to raise money! That sounds promising. Who can we get to perform?

Brian It would be great to get someone like Luke Hutchison, the greatest singer of all time.

Don I think we're shooting too high. I was thinking more like a local band.

Stan I've got it. My sister knows some local bands from this area. Maybe we can get a few of them to perform.

Don That would be great.

Brian I like how this is shaping up. We're out of time, but let's meet again on Friday to hammer out the details. Thanks everybody.

Comprehension Questions

Q1. What is the purpose of this meeting?
Q2. Who seems to be chairing this meeting?
Q3. What is the meaning of "a benefit performance"?
Q4. What do you think they will be focusing on at the next meeting?

3. Language Practice

A Chunks & Chew

Complete the sentences with the appropriate words and expressions from the dialogue.

- ☐ called a meeting
- ☐ a ballpark figure
- ☐ come up with
- ☐ (be) shaping up
- ☐ hammer / out

① Nobody could _____ a satisfactory explanation for the accident.
② We'd been arguing about the issue for weeks, so the four of us got together to _____ it _____.
③ The mayor _____ to discuss the problems.
④ This group of summer interns is _____ to be one of the best we've ever hired.
⑤ Can you give us _____ of our projected losses in the next quarter?

B Key Patterns

Here are some key patterns that you can use when exchanging opinions.

① _____ in danger of _____ ?
- The employees are / losing their jobs
- Frogs are / becoming extinct
- We are / losing our free speech

② It/That would be great _____.
- to see you again
- if you could make it to the team gathering tonight
- if we could go to Manchester as well

③ I like how _____.
- it all worked out for the team
- this turned out okay
- he gets things done

Business Basics

Communication Style: Direct vs. Indirect

In your communication toolbox, direct and indirect skills are like a hammer and screwdriver: both are helpful, but you need to use the right tool at the right time. The exercise below will help you define the differences. In the underlined space, write "Indirect" if you think it applies to a culture where communication is indirect, or "Direct" if communication is direct.

1. .... "Yes" means "Yes"
2. .... "Yes" means "I hear you"
3. .... People are reluctant to say no.
4. .... You have to read between the lines.
5. .... Use of intermediaries or third parties is frequent.
6. .... It's okay to disagree with your boss at a meeting.
7. .... People engage in small talk before getting down to business.
8. .... Business first, then small talk.
9. .... It's best to tell it like it is.

[Answers]
(1) Direct, (2) Indirect, (3) Indirect, (4) Indirect, (5) Indirect, (6) Direct, (7) Indirect, (8) Direct, (9) Direct

4. Role Plays

Read each situation and role play with your partner.

• 01 Situation

You work for a merchandising company. Your team invites related parties to an informative meeting for the next quarter. Organize a small meeting to prepare for the informative meeting and set an agenda for the meeting.

• 02 Situation

For a month, you have been waiting for an order of goods for the upcoming holiday season. You just got a call from the supplier. He/she says shipping's been delayed because of production problems. Call for an urgent problem-solving meeting and check with the supplier for suggestions.

• 03 Situation

There is serious tension between you and your colleague because you two have different work styles. You've been tiptoeing around the issue and suffering from declining productivity. You finally decided to face it and confront your colleague. Talk to him/her to bring out the problem.

5. Discussion

Discuss the following questions in detail.

1. Do you have a difficult time expressing yourself in a meeting?
2. Have you ever felt like you were in competition with your co-workers while participating in a meeting?
3. Would you agree with someone in a meeting because you felt intimidated?
4. What type of meeting is easier to express your ideas and thoughts (e.g., small meetings vs. large meetings)? Why?
5. What are some good tips to express your opinions effectively at work?

One Point Lesson

Raise vs. Rise

 The cost of living has raisen by 20% this year.

 The cost of living has risen by 20% this year.

Both "raise" and "rise" can mean "to move upwards," but they are not interchangeable. "Rise" is an intransitive verb, and "raise" is a transitive verb.
"Raise" requires an object to cause the motion. It is a transitive verb and refers to something being moved to a higher position or something being improved. For example, we can say: "Please raise your hand if you want to speak."

On the other hand, "rise" is used to describe a person, animal, or something moving upwards by itself (to ascend, go up). It is an intransitive verb, and it does not take an object. We say: "The sun rises in the morning."

LESSON 11 / Exchanging Opinions 57

6. Business Skills - Interactive Meeting Skills

It is typical to offer opinions on projects, information, or deadlines. Management expects you to give your opinion; otherwise, you're not considered a valuable employee. However, it's still important to respect work relationships without making someone angry or upset. Here are some expressions often used to politely disagree, offer a different opinion, appropriately interrupt someone, or clarify a point.

Categorizing — Look at the expressions and write the numbers in the appropriate situations below to indicate where they should be used.

① I understand how you feel, but I believe we need a different approach because....
② I get your point; however, I think another method would work better, for example....
③ I see what you mean, but unfortunately it's not possible to do that because....
④ I see you worked very hard on this; however, it's not what was needed for this project.
⑤ You are a diligent employee, but this format doesn't meet our needs.
⑥ I understand what you tried to do here, and I applaud the effort, but we can't use it.
⑦ Do I understand you correctly that...?
⑧ Are saying...?
⑨ Can you explain that in more simple terms?
⑩ Can I come in here?
⑪ If you don't mind, may I make a comment here?
⑫ If I may, I need to point out something at this time.

Clarifying a point

Offering a different opinion

Politely disagreeing

Interrupting

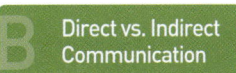
Direct vs. Indirect Communication — In this activity, you are presented with a series of six direct statements. Rephrase them to make them more indirect.

	Direct	Indirect
1	I don't think that's a good idea.	
2	That's not the point.	
3	I think we should do (something)...	
4	Those figures are not accurate.	
5	You're doing that wrong.	
6	I don't agree.	

Wrapping Up!

▶ 3 new words from this lesson

▶ 3 new expressions from this lesson

▶ 3 things to remember

Lesson 12
Following Up

Learning Objectives
After completing this lesson, you will be able to...
- follow up plans after a meeting and develop a business relationship by e-mail.
- make sure of what is discussed to follow up afterward.

OVERVIEW
☐ Warm Up Activities
☐ Useful Expressions
☐ Dialogue
☐ Language Practice
☐ Business Basics
☐ Role Plays
☐ Discussion
☐ One Point Lesson
☐ Business Skills
☐ Business Manner & Etiquette

1. Warm Up Activities

A Talk about the questions.

1. Do you usually follow up on phone calls with written confirmation?
2. How does your team follow through on ideas after a brainstorming meeting?
3. Do you usually make time to follow up after you have a meeting with customers?

B Discuss the following questions with a partner.

Look at the situation and role play with your classmates.

"When You Should Follow Something Up"

Wendy just got back from a business trip to Chicago. Matt introduces Mr. Zimmerman to Wendy. Mr. Zimmerman is visiting this company to attend a review conference. Matt asks Wendy to have dinner together, but Wendy have something to follow up after her business trip.

- **Wendy Nelson**: Financial Consultant, M&M Consulting Group
- **Matt Reed**: Junior Financial Consultant, M&M Consulting Group
- **Rick Zimmerman**: Project Manager, T&S Group

Useful Expressions

A Positive Comments

ⓐ It's been great meeting with you.
ⓑ The same for me.

ⓐ Everything was great.
ⓑ I'm pleased you enjoyed it.

ⓐ We've had a wonderful time.
ⓑ I'm glad you found it interesting.

B Future Contact
- I hope we'll see you again soon.
- I look forward to seeing you next month.

C Today's Expressions

Match the expressions (1-4) with the similar meanings (a-d).

① They are on the cutting edge.
② He is flying out tonight at 9 p.m.
③ She just got back from a business trip.
④ I'm surprised that someone so talented is also so modest.

☐ a. She has just returned from a business trip.
☐ b. They just discovered and tried new techniques.
☐ c. He surprised me with his humble attitude.
☐ d. He has a flight tonight at 9 p.m.

LESSON 12 /Following Up 59

2. Dialogue
Read the dialogue and answer the questions with a partner.

Follow-up Meetings

Matt Ms. Nelson. I thought you were on a business trip to Chicago?

Wendy I was. I just got back this morning.

Matt I see. Was your trip a success?

Wendy Yes, it was. I was able to get a deal signed that should bring in substantial revenue.

Matt Great! I'm glad everything panned out. Oh, by the way, this is Mr. Rick Zimmerman from T&S Group. They were ranked one of the best up-and-coming energy companies for three consecutive years. He is here to streamline the follow-up review process of the current project.

Wendy How do you do, Mr. Zimmerman?

Mr.Zimmerman How do you do? It's a pleasure to meet you.

Matt Mr. Zimmerman is one of our top clients. They're right there on the cutting edge. I'm sure you'll be reading about some of their breakthroughs in the coming months.

Mr.Zimmerman Well, we still have some work cut out for us. I wouldn't toot our horn just yet.

Matt Oh, you're just being modest. By the way, We're going to have dinner at Ruby Friday after the review. Can you join us?

Wendy I'm afraid not. I have to meet with our CFO to discuss our present deal. We also need to discuss the details on how to follow through afterward. Can I take a rain check?

Matt Sure. Well, good luck with your meeting.

comprehension Questions
Q1. What company does Mr. Zimmerman work for?

Q2. What was the purpose of Wendy's visit to Chicago?

Q3. What are Matt and Mr. Zimmerman going to discuss in the meeting?

3. Language Practice

A Chunks & Chew
Complete the sentences with the appropriate words and expressions from the dialogue.

- ☐ up-and-coming
- ☐ cut out for
- ☐ pan out
- ☐ take a rain check
- ☐ toot / horn

① He's really got his work _____ him.

② Do you mind if I _____ on that drink?

③ Jen doesn't like to _____ her own _____, but she is the best lawyer in the firm.

④ The summer exhibition has a major focus on young _____ talent.

⑤ I didn't know that the deal would _____.

B Key Patterns
Here are some key patterns that you can use when having a conversation at work.

① _____ on the cutting edge _____.
- These models are / of computer design
- Healthy Hospital is / of medical technology
- The technology is right / and not available to the public yet

② _____ (be) just being + adjective
- You are / nice.
- She is / too sensitive.
- Is he / modest?

③ Good luck in/on/with _____.
- your interview tomorrow
- your exam
- the competition

Business Basics

Regular Follow Up Can Increase Sales

In a recent new-business meeting, a potential client pointed out a trait we try to instill in all of our employees: the ability to provide timely and effective follow-up.

The National Sales Association statics show:	How to follow up effectively
- 2% of sales are made on the 1st contact - 3% of sales are made on the 2nd contact - 5% of sales are made on the 3rd contact - 10% of sales are made on the 4th contact - 80% of sales are made on the 5th-12th contact	- Don't beat around the bush. Be direct and ask for what you want. - Be sensitive to schedules and try to consider the best time to reach that person. - Don't just call to call. Each follow-up call you make should provide new value and not be done just to check in or to meet a call quota.

4. Role Plays

Read each situation and role play with your partner.

01 You're working for an international company. The headquarters is in the US. Your office is located in Japan. Your local team had a video conference with the marketing team at the headquarters, and they gave you a task to outline the marketing strategy to sell products in your country. You and your team members have a follow-up meeting to discuss the matter. You should lead the meeting.

02 Your team just finished a conference call. Now your team would like to review the meeting after taking notes during the conference call. Lead a short follow-up meeting and try to reach consensus.

03 You had a meeting with a client and found out that you both like Indian food. You want to have a lunch meeting (at an Indian restaurant) with the client and follow up the work/project. Call him/her and suggest having a meeting.

5. Discussion

Discuss the following questions in detail.

1. How do you usually follow up important meetings with clients?
2. What are the advantages of a follow-up e-mail?
3. You meet and spend time with a dozen people at a conference and diligently take all of their business cards. How do you follow up with them within the next few days?

One Point Lesson

Day after day vs. Day by day

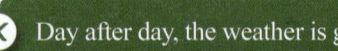 Day after day, the weather is getting warmer.

 Day by day, the weather is getting warmer

"Day after day" means "repeatedly" or "continuously" for many days, especially in a boring or unpleasant way. We could say, "I get fed up with listening to their complaints day after day."

However, "day by day" means "gradually" or "progressively." We usually say, "The weather is getting warmer day by day" or "Their love grew day by day."

6. Business Skills - Following Up by E-mail

What you say in an e-mail and how you say it depend on the type of message and who's receiving it. If you are writing to a new client or to your boss, it will be more formal. An e-mail to a long-term client or friend will use much more casual language.

A Common e-mail vocabulary

Fill in the blanks with the appropriate e-mail vocabulary.

| ASAP | appreciate | request | satisfactory | inquiry |
| interest | know | send | received | attachment |

1. I'm sending you the price list in the _____.
2. I'd _____ a reply ASAP.
3. Let me _____ if you need any more help.
4. I would like to _____ a catalogue of your products.
5. Please answer _____.
6. I hope you find this _____ to your needs.
7. Your _____ is being processed.
8. Thank you for your _____.
9. Can you _____ me the information at your earliest convenience?
10. We _____ your payment yesterday.

B Formal and informal e-mail phrases

Use the language below to complete the table.

1. Can you help?
2. We hope you are happy with us.
3. Let us know if you need any more help.
4. Please answer ASAP.
5. I'm sending you the ... in an attachment.
6. I'm sending you....
7. We are working on your request....
8. Can you send me...?

More Formal	Less Formal
Requesting information	
• I'd appreciate a reply as soon as possible.	
• Would you be able to help me...?	
• Could you please send me...?	
Replies	
• Please find the ... in an attachment.	
• I'm pleased to send you....	
• Please do not hesitate to contact us if you require further assistance.	
• We hope you find this satisfactory.	
• Your request is being processed.	

E-MAIL ETIQUETTE

Business Manner & Etiquette

☑ **Keep it short** - Easy to read, short and clear. Shrink sentences and list items.

☑ **Reply to all** – Check everyone relevant is included. Carbon copy those who don't need to take action, but need to know how it is going on.

☑ **Descriptive subject** – The subject of an e-mail describes its contents and attachments in a short sentence.

☑ **Searchable e-mails** – Think about which keywords you would search in order to help you find the e-mail easily even after several months.

☑ **Reply with History** – If there is already a related e-mail, reply to it. If it has a different subject, create a new one.

Wrapping Up!

▶ 3 new words from this lesson

▶ 3 new expressions from this lesson

▶ 3 things to remember

Business Practice 1

03 Outsourcing Customer Service

◎ Background

Web.com is a medium-sized Web hosting and Internet services provider located in Brookfield, Connecticut that helps small businesses succeed online. They have over 3 million customers and have been in business since 1996. Their areas of greatest importance include: offering flexible and customizable solutions and being a completely customer-focused organization. Due to the technical nature of their business (and often not-so-technical customers), clients can require a lot of attention and personal care.

An early decision was to offer live sales and technical support 24 hours a day, 365 days a year. However, taking orders from a thousand new customers every day is not something for the faint of heart or the ill-prepared. It requires time and patience, a tremendous devotion to service and a highly skilled team of professionals.

◎ Outsourcing Customer Service

Read the passage from Web.com. Then answer the following questions.

> We wrestled with the decision to outsource our customer support for over a year. We researched quite extensively, and after spinning out the costs, we decided to do it. In doing our homework, we learned that it costs less than in the US. The decision seemed like a no-brainer, so we selected a company in Bangalore, India. We thought we were off to a good start, but we experienced many problems due to cultural differences. First, we expected our representatives to talk as long as necessary to solve the customers' problems. But in India, there is less focus on problem solving and more on meeting their call center time limits. For example, if they made a call shorter, they were rewarded for it. Shorter call times don't necessarily make happier customers. The greatest problem we faced was the cultural clash.
>
> There's a cultural communication gap.
>
> The word "revert," for example, means one thing in India and another in Oklahoma. We tried to use a "yes/no" procedure, but it didn't work and it was a mess. These communication misunderstandings led us back to Connecticut. Initially, we were optimistic about outsourcing, but in the end, we found we were losing customer service. What's more, now communication across our different departments has dramatically improved. The staff receives continual in-house training on the products and services that we offer, and our customers are happy.

- Why is customer service so important?
- What does "outsourced" mean?
- What was the reason for outsourcing?
- Did it increase the profits of web.com?
- What were the problems?
- Why do you think it's different in India?
- What did web.com do to improve their service in the US?

CASE STUDY 03

◎ Analyze

Ⓐ Barriers to Communication

The lack of effective communication results in the loss of valuable time, resources, materials and even life. The following barriers may cause a simple communication gap or a total failure of communication.

1	Physical Environmental Barriers Caused by Distance, Noise, etc.
2	Barriers Caused by Wrong Choice of Medium
3	Semantic Barriers Caused by Varied Connotative Meanings
4	Cultural Barriers Caused by Diversity of Cultures
5	Psychological Barriers Caused by Moods, Attitudes, Relationships
6	Barriers Caused by Varying Perceptions of Reality
7	Barriers Caused by Levels of Understanding and Comprehension

▶ Interview your partner about some experience of communication gap due to one of the reasons.

....

....

▶ Which barriers do you think we typically experience in the workplace? Rate their importance.

....

▶ What efforts do you make to prevent failing communication?

....

Ⓑ Ways to Prevent Communication Breakdown

Work in small groups. You are a member of the in-house training group of web.com. Hold a meeting to propose ideas for ways to avoid communication breakdown.

01. ....

02. ....

03. ....

◎ Presentation

You are managers of a cell phone distributor who has been affected the downturn of the economy. You are losing money; you have to make some changes in your business. Discuss ways you can cut costs by outsourcing some parts of your business in other countries and make the business plan.
Then, make a related presentation to the stakeholders and your boss. You need to expect a possible communication barrier between the H.Q. and the agencies; be ready to suggest some creative and useful ways to prevent communication breakdown or miscommunication.

Bullet Points of Your Presentation

* ....

* ....

* ....

Lesson 13
Going on a Business Trip

Learning Objectives

After completing this lesson, you will be able to...
- plan a business trip and know how to book airline tickets and make hotel reservations.
- know how to behave appropriately on a business trip.

OVERVIEW
☐ Warm Up Activities
☐ Useful Expressions
☐ Dialogue
☐ Language Practice
☐ Business Basics
☐ Role Plays
☐ Discussion
☐ One Point Lesson
☐ Business Skills

1. Warm Up Activities

A Talk about the questions.

1. When you go on a business trip, what information do you need to find out?
2. How do you pack for a business trip? Do you usually pack light?
3. Which one do you prefer – domestic or international business trips?

B Discuss the following questions with a partner.

Look at the situation and role play with your classmates.

"Before going on a business trip"

Todd decided to have Brian go on a business trip to Seattle to get problems fixed at SMA Securities, one of their major clients.

- **Todd Smith**: Senior Manager, Micro Systems Management Company
- **Brian**: Senior staff member, Micro Systems Management Company

Useful Expressions

A Reservation
- Are there seats on Monday's flight?
- Please confirm your reservation in advance.
- I'd like to cancel my reservation.

B Flight
- Will the flight leave on time?
- Which gate are we boarding from?
- Do I have to declare my video camera?
- How early should I check in before take off?

C Today's Expressions

Match the expressions (1-4) with the similar meanings (a-d).

① He hasn't arrived yet, but not to worry. He'll be here shortly.
② Are you busy at the moment?
③ We're well aware of the fact that the company is losing money.
④ I tried to get my points across to my boss.

☐ a. I tried to convince my boss that my points actually make sense.
☐ b. He is running a little late, but I'm not worried because he'll be here in no time.
☐ c. Is this a good time to talk?
☐ d. We all realize that the company is going under.

2. Dialogue
Read the dialogue and answer the questions with a partner.

Last-Minute Decision on a Business Trip

Brian Mr. Smith, are you busy at the moment?

Todd A little, but not to worry. What's up?

Brian Rich Thornton from SMA Securities just called me. They have been having problems with their system. It doesn't seem to be very compatible with their browsers.

Todd Is it something we need to act on right away?

Brian Most definitely. To be frank, I think you should let me fly out to Seattle to act right on it. You don't want to lose SMA Securities, right?

Todd Yeah, can you put it all down in an e-mail and send it to me right away? Also, I need you to send me the travel expense report that you haven't submitted yet after the last business trip to Tokyo. Mindy from the Finance Department has been asking me for it. They need to file it away before they start to work on the monthly closing.

Brian Yes, I am well aware of that. I've just been snowed under with work for the whole week. I think some of the receipts might not be available, but I will make sure to get it done by 5 p.m.

Todd Sounds good. Back to SMA Securities – don't forget to explain what the most pressing issues are and how we can solve them right away.

Brian Sure, sir. I'll get that across to you in a jiffy! Thanks.

Comprehension Questions

Q1. Why does Brian have to go to Seattle?

Q2. What kinds of problems has SMA Securities been having lately?

Q3. What does Brian need to explain in his e-mail?

3. Language Practice

A Chunks & Chew
Complete the sentences with the appropriate words and expressions from the dialogue.

☐ acting on
☐ (be) filed away
☐ put / down
☐ (be) snowed under with
☐ in a jiffy

① The vice president asked the staff to _____ all the complaints _____ on paper.
② We are _____ applications for the job.
③ Call her if you have any problems. She will get it fixed _____!
④ They were _____ the instructions of senior managers.
⑤ All the relevant documents are _____ with the property deeds.

B Key Patterns
Here are some key patterns that you can use when talking about your business trip.

① Don't forget to _____ .
- ask them for the unemployment pay
- contact your seller with any questions about payment
- RSVP right way

② To be frank, _____ .
- I'm not happy with the decision at all
- I'm very disappointed with your behavior
- I'm not sure you have the experience to do the job well

③ _____ might not be available _____ .
- Some files / to download
- Rick / for a while
- The funds that you deposit / to you immediately

Business Basics

How to Behave Appropriately on a Business Trip

Whether this will be your first or your thousandth business trip, you should be conscious of conduct that is considered proper during your absence from the office. As a representative of your company, you need to know how to behave appropriately on a business trip.

01 Dress professionally during the entire trip. Your attire should reflect the fact that you are on a business trip, whether you are on a plane, on a golf course, or in a conference room.

02 Use proper business language. Even though some business trips may include more casual situations, such as lunch, dinner, or even golf, keep in mind that you are still representing your company. Like the old saying goes: "Loose lips sink ships."

03 Brush up on table manners and the basics of business etiquette before you go. This may help you avoid an embarrassing gaffe while on your trip.

04 Save all receipts from your trip so you can easily determine your expenses when you return.

05 Conduct yourself with grace and decorum at all times. If you are uncertain about these terms, consider buying a book on business etiquette for some light reading while on the plane.

4. Role Plays

Read each situation and role play with your partner.

• 01 Situation

You went to business trip last month to Colombia. You are supposed to submit a travel expense report to get business trip expenses reimbursed by the end of this month. Discuss with your colleague what items are needed in a travel expense report.

• 02 Situation

You are a businessperson. You have an important business meeting in Paris next Thursday. You need a roundtrip ticket to Paris before Thursday. You are traveling alone, and you would prefer a business class ticket since your boss is paying for the ticket. You would like to return the following Monday. Call a travel agent to book your ticket.

• 03 Situation

You are traveling to London to attend a business meeting. You experience intercultural barriers throughout the trip and try to adjust to different cultural communication patterns. Strike up a conversation with the other attendees around you before the meeting starts and talk about intercultural barriers.

5. Discussion

Discuss the following questions in detail.

1. What is your travel-friendly business attire?
2. Do you think dressing smart helps you close the deal and impress your colleagues or clients?
3. Do you have a job that requires traveling on business trips? How often?
4. Have you ever had any difficulty travelling on business trips? How did you deal with the situation?
5. What can be the hardest part of business trips, especially long-term travel?

One Point Lesson

Travel vs. Trip

 Jamie is planning a two-week travel to Eastern Europe next month.

 Jamie is planning a two-week trip to Eastern Europe next month.

"Travel" is generally used as a verb meaning to go somewhere or to move from place to place. It is the general activity of moving about the world. When you travel to a place that is far away or to a place that you visit regularly, you "go on/make a journey."

When you go to a place and come back again, especially for a short visit, you go on/make/take a trip. "Trip" is a noun meaning a journey, for business or pleasure. We usually use "take a trip."

6. Business Skills - Business Trip & Business Etiquette

Business travel can be very stressful for travelers. Travelers are concerned about traveling safely without incident, and they also worry about making a positive business impression. Successful business travel requires preparation. A well-planned business trip allows you to focus on the business portion of the trip without worrying about the travel arrangements.

A Making a Reservation

Work in pairs. Take turns being the ticket agent and traveler. Change location and date and role plays with your partner.

A) Airline (Here are two options.)

Airline	Direct/Stopover	Departure Time	Departure Time	Price
Delta	Direct	9:10 AM	8:40 PM	$985.00
Chrystal	Stopover	3:30 PM	5:15 AM	$760.00

B) Hotel

City	Check-in date	Single/Double	Check-out date/Number of nights	Smoking/Non-smoking
Boston	Feb 18th	single	Feb 20th, 2	non-smoking
Shanghai	Mar 1st	double	Mar 5th, 4	smoking
San Francisco	June 20th	double	June 23rd, 3	non-smoking

- Boston flying February 18th, returning Feb 20th.
- Shanghai flying March 1st, returning March 5th.
- San Francisco flying June 20th, returning June 23rd

B Meeting New Clients

Business etiquette is different for every culture, from handshaking to introductions. Take the following quiz to see what's appropriate. Afterward, discuss in pairs what's common in your county's business culture and how it's different from others.

1. It is appropriate to stand close to a business contact and frequently touch his/her arm while talking.
   ⓐ True ⓑ False

2. The manager you are meeting with (on your overseas business trip) brings in the office sales team for introductions. You:
   ⓐ Smile and nod, but say nothing.
   ⓑ Stand up, establish eye contact, smile, and give each team member a firm handshake.
   ⓒ Give him a "high five."
   ⓓ Shake the hands of only the men.

3. You have a meeting with someone scheduled for 10:00 a.m. It's now 10:05, and you have been waiting since 9:45. You've told the receptionist who you are supposed to meet. You want to make sure the person knows you're there. What do you do?
   ⓐ Look inside his office and say, "Excuse me, I'm waiting for you. When will you come out?"
   ⓑ Stand near the door of his office where he will see you.
   ⓒ Patiently continue to sit and wait. The receptionist has told him; he'll be out as soon as he can.

4. After a meeting with a contact, in order to express your thanks, it is appropriate to:
   ⓐ Drop by the office and give him/her a hot cup of coffee.
   ⓑ Send a dozen red roses to his/her home.
   ⓒ Send a thank you letter.
   ⓓ Do research and find out what's appropriate for that culture.

5. When meeting a contact of the opposite sex, the man should wait for the woman to initiate the handshake.
   ⓐ True ⓑ False

6. When breaking the ice with a new contact at the beginning of a meeting, it is appropriate to discuss such things as age, the weather, religion, politics, and traffic.
   ⓐ True ⓑ False

7. It is acceptable to leave your cell phone on during overseas business meetings and answer it when it rings.
   ⓐ True ⓑ False

Wrapping Up!

▶ 3 new words from this lesson

▶ 3 new expressions from this lesson

▶ 3 things to remember

Lesson 14
Understanding Cultural Diversity

Learning Objectives
After completing this lesson, you will be able to...
- describe your overseas experience and cultural differences you've experienced.
- get information about business culture and etiquette.

OVERVIEW
☐ Warm Up Activities
☐ Useful Expressions
☐ Dialogue
☐ Language Practice
☐ Business Basics
☐ Role Plays
☐ Discussion
☐ One Point Lesson
☐ Business Skills

1. Warm Up Activities

A Discuss the following questions with a partner.

1. Have you ever experienced cultural differences while you were working with foreign clients or colleagues?
2. Do you prefer to talk to people from your own culture instead of people from other cultures?
3. What customs or social rules in your country could cause cultural shocks for foreign colleagues or clients?

B Today's situation

Look at the situation and role play with your classmates.

"When you talk about cultural differences"

Jack is having a conversation with his coworker, Robert, during a coffee break. Jack asks some questions about his business trip along with cultural differences in Sweden.

- **Jack**: Senior production engineer, Team A
- **Robert**: Senior production engineer, Team B

Useful Expressions

A Overseas Experience

ⓐ Have you ever been to the United States?
ⓑ Yes, I have. / No, I've never been to the United States.

B Social Events

ⓐ How do you celebrate birthdays in the United States?
ⓑ We celebrate with family and usually have a cake with candles on it.

C Today's Expressions

Match the expressions (1-4) with the similar meanings (a-d).

① They prefer to be direct in business.
② I'd like to put you in charge of reviewing the minutes.
③ Have you ever been to Sweden before?
④ I will take your word for it.

☐ a. Is this your first time visiting Sweden?
☐ b. They like to be straightforward when it comes to doing business.
☐ c. I believe what you are telling me now is true.
☐ d. Can you be responsible for reviewing the minutes?

2. Dialogue
Read the dialogue and answer the questions with a partner.

Business Culture in Sweden

Robert Jack, I heard you are going to Sweden on business.

Jack Yes, my team decided to put me in charge of the upcoming project. Robert, you've been there before, haven't you? Can you give me some advice about the culture? This is my first visit, and I don't want to make mistakes.

Robert How long are you going to stay there?

Jack About a month. My business trip is four weeks long.

Robert Then, you shouldn't need a visa, but just in case, call the local Swedish embassy to check.

Jack Can they speak English?

Robert Yes. Most Swedes speak very good English.

Jack Now that you mention it, I've been trying to brush up on my English.

Robert It is also a good idea to learn some Swedish phrases such as "please" and "thank you."

Jack How about making appointments?

Robert Umm ... It is good to make appointments at least two weeks in advance. Also, you need to be punctual for all business and social appointments. This is very important to Swedish people.

Jack Okay, I'll take your word for it. Anything else?

Robert During the meeting, it isn't necessary to talk if you don't have anything to say. Swedes prefer to be direct in business, so it isn't a good idea to interrupt. So, in meetings and negotiations, it is important to keep calm. Don't get emotional. Okay?

Jack Got it. Thank you so much, Robert!

comprehension Questions
Q1. How long will Jack stay in Sweden?
Q2. If Jack has some problem with his visa, where should he call?
Q3. What phrases would be good to learn when visiting Sweden?

3. Language Practice

A Chunks & Chew
Complete the sentences with the appropriate words and expressions from the dialogue.

- ☐ (be) put in charge of
- ☐ give advice
- ☐ make mistakes
- ☐ in advance
- ☐ brush up on

① I _____, but I try to learn afterward.
② The bill isn't due for a month, but I paid it _____.
③ My German is weak. I'd better _____ it.
④ He was subsequently _____ the whole project.
⑤ Please _____ on a new hire.

B Key Patterns
Here are some key patterns that you can use when talking about cultural diversity.

① **Now that _____.**
- you are here, you might as well stay for the meeting
- you mention it, I did see a strange man outside
- you've gotten a promotion, what are you going to do first?

② **_____ make an appointment _____**
- I need to / at the social security office.
- Can I / with a specific banker?
- Make sure that you / in advance.

③ **It isn't necessary to _____.**
- be perfect in order to be successful
- have relatives in Tokyo
- make friends with everyone before you start the project

Business Basics

Culture Shock and Adjustment

When you move to a different country, you may experience some form of culture shock. Culture shock refers to the feelings of anxiety, surprise, uncertainty, confusion, etc. that you experience when you live in a different cultural or social environment. You will probably dislike some aspects of the culture. This is completely normal. Almost everyone experiences culture shock in some way. Some people are affected more seriously than others.

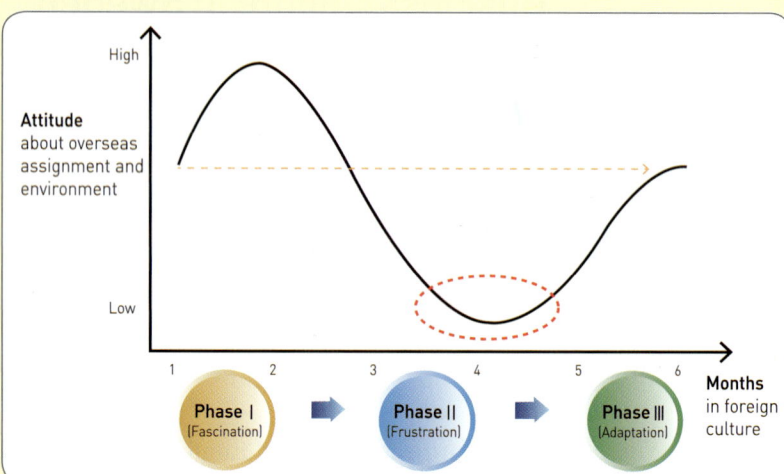

4. Role Plays

Read each situation and role play with your partner.

Situation 01: You have a new company director, who came from another country. The new company director has organized a team-building exercise this weekend. The event is paint ball. You don't understand why you have to spend weekend with co-workers, and want to have time with your family. At the same time, however, you don't want to be seen as a non-team-player. Ask your colleagues for advice.

Situation 02: Weeks ago, you received a printed invitation to a breakfast seminar at a hotel. You RSVP'd but overlooked that it said the dress code was business attire. You enter the conference room in business-casual clothes (khakis and a collared shirt), only to find everyone in suits. Talk to your colleague and find a solution.

Situation 03: You are at a restaurant in the US. The waiter is rude, and the food is mediocre. You don't want to leave a tip, but your foreign colleague says you ought to because it's the custom. Tell her/him about your culture to describe the different cultural characteristics.

5. Discussion

Discuss the following questions in detail.

1. Are the people of your country well-mannered compared to other nationalities?
2. Have you ever thought about an overseas job hunt? How confident are you of getting hired overseas?
3. What are some international business strategies to get off to a good start when making the initial contact with an international client?
4. In some cultures, men do not talk directly to women, and they avoid making eye contact with women. How would this affect international business?

One Point Lesson

Continuously vs. Continually

❌ The meeting was continuously interrupted.

◎ The meeting was continually interrupted.

Both words, continually and continuously, are often used interchangeably. However, they are used differently in certain contexts.

"Continually" means "happening repeatedly" over a long period of time, especially in a way that you find annoying. We could say, "That telephone has been ringing continually." However, "continuously" indicates duration that continues over a long period time without any break or interruption. We normally say, "A line of cars stretched continuously down the motorway."

LESSON 14 / Understanding Cultural Diversity 71

6. Business Skills - Cultural Diversity & Cultural Values

Learning about a country's culture can help you have good working relations when doing business in other countries. Using and understanding the local etiquette can be more valuable than learning the language.

A Cultural Values

1) Rate the following values from 1 to 10 (1 being unimportant, 5 being somewhat important, and 10 being extremely important). Then discuss your choices with your partner.
2) What are some aspects of your culture that you feel should change?
3) Is cultural change a good or bad thing?
4) What do you think are the strongest aspects of your culture?

Openness to new ideas		Freedom of expression	
Honesty		Importance of education	
Respect for authority		Hard work	
Human rights		Importance of individual	
Importance of time		Harmony	
Importance of religion		Helping others	

B Cultural Diversity

Look at the followings and find out which country each paragraph explains. Then, answer the questions related to each explanation.

Greeks, Japan, China, Thailand, Sweden

1) Verbal Communication

* In _____, people feel that "no" is an impolite word, and will sometimes say "yes" to avoid offending people. What they really mean is "I understand what you're saying," not "I agree."

Question) Why do you think "no" can be impolite? What about in your country?

2) Gestures

* Even the movement of your head can be misunderstood. _____ use an upward nod of the head to say "no," and tilting their heads from side to side means "yes." But, the younger generation uses a Western way to communicate no when they move their head.

Question) What body movements are used to say yes and no in your culture?

3) Physical Touch

* In _____, don't touch or pass anything over a person's head, as in the culture the head is sacred. However, people often stand very close and touch each other on the arm when talking.

Question) Are there some body movements that are considered offensive and shouldn't be done? What are they?

4) At a Restaurant

* In _____, taste everything you're offered during meals – but never clear your plate as your host will assume you're still hungry. Don't talk business during meals.
* Toasting in _____ involves eye contact but no glass-touching. A "skol" and a nod to everyone will do the trick.
* Don't say no to a glass of baiju, the liquor of choice that is served at all formal dinners. But drink with restraint: draining your glass will result in a refill. Leaving it half-full is perfectly acceptable in _____.

Question) What about in your country? Is there any specific culture you should follow when you have a meal at a restaurant?

Wrapping Up!

▶ 3 new words from this lesson

▶ 3 new expressions from this lesson

▶ 3 things to remember

Lesson 15
Different Communication Styles

Learning Objectives

After completing this lesson, you will be able to...
- understand different communication styles depending on cultures.
- avoid making cultural mistakes when communicating.

OVERVIEW
☐ Warm Up Activities
☐ Useful Expressions
☐ Dialogue
☐ Language Practice
☐ Business Basics
☐ Role Plays
☐ Discussion
☐ One Point Lesson
☐ Business Skills

1. Warm Up Activities

A Discuss the following questions with a partner.

1. Have you ever made cultural mistakes before, especially at work?
2. What is the worst communication problem you've ever experienced with your boss?
3. Have you had an opportunity to work with a foreign boss? If yes, how did you overcome communication barriers?

B Today's situation

Look at the situation and role play with your classmates.

"When you talk about cultural mistakes"

Annette and Sean start a conversation in the break room. Annette tells Sean about what Sarah has been up to. Sean points out their cultural misunderstanding.

- **Annette, Sean, Sarah:**
  Senior staff members, Process Measurement & Control Division

Useful Expressions

A Clarifying and Confirming in a Meeting

- Going back to what you just said about ..., could you clarify what you mean?
- Correct me if I'm wrong, but do you mean...?
- I'm sorry; could you go over that again?
- What exactly do you mean by...?

B Today's Expressions

Match the expressions (1-5) with the similar meanings (a-e).

① Someone finally pointed out that we had to be up early for work.
② Flexibility is essential to open-minded leaders.
③ Try to look at it from his point of view.
④ Her boss is trying to do her a favor.
⑤ Now you're talking!

____ a. Can you try to put yourself in his shoes?
____ b. We realized that we had to be back at work early tomorrow.
____ c. Now you are saying the right things.
____ d. Good leaders should keep an open mind and listen to those that have different viewpoints.
____ e. He is trying to do it to help her out.

LESSON 15 / Different Communication Styles

2. Dialogue
Read the dialogue and answer the questions with a partner.

Be Open-Minded and Embrace Cultural Differences

Annette Sean, did you hear what happened to Sarah?

Sean No, what happened?

Annette Her boss asked her to move to the Tech Support Team. Since then, shes' been so bummed out.

Sean Why is she bummed out?

Annette Think about it! Why would your boss want to transfer you to another division unless you're a pain in his neck? Sarah always thought her boss played favorites and that she was always chosen for the great tasks.

Sean Are you serious? I think it's all a misunderstanding. Isn't her boss from the States?

Annette Yes, I think he's from Seattle.

Sean Her boss wants to give her a great opportunity to widen her horizons by experiencing something different. He wouldn't have suggested that if he hadn't had faith in her.

Annette Hmm, what makes you say that?

Sean Try to look at it from his point of view. In his culture, people generally change jobs within the same industry because it gives them a broader base of experience. They view a job change as a way of promoting themselves to a better position. Her boss is trying to do her a favor.

Annette Wow, now that you mention it, it was just a cultural misunderstanding.

Sean Now you're talking!

Comprehension Questions
- **Q1.** What kind of issue has Sarah been struggling with?
- **Q2.** Why is Sarah so disappointed with her boss?
- **Q3.** What kind of cultural difference are they talking about?
- **Q4.** What is Sarah's point of view on this?

3. Language Practice

A Chunks & Chew
Complete the sentences with the appropriate words and expressions from the dialogue.

- ☐ (be) bummed out
- ☐ playing favorites
- ☐ widened our horizons
- ☐ have faith in
- ☐ a pain in the neck

① We _____ you and know you can do the job well.
② This trip to the Far East has _____ .
③ The mayor said he wasn't _____ in the presidential campaign.
④ Everybody was totally _____ because I wasn't there.
⑤ This tax form is _____ .

B Key Patterns
Here are some key patterns that you can use when talking about culture and communication styles.

① Did you hear _____ ?
- the news about the bankers
- what the boss did
- that we are getting iPads

② _____ views someone as _____ .
- Everyone / my sister / sweet and fragile
- My boss still / me / very young and green
- The student / school / being pertinent to his future life

③ _____ chosen for _____ .
- The software company was / the project.
- Why was this name / your company?
- Salt Lake City was once / the Winter Olympics.

Business Basics

Nonverbal Communication

A well-known communication studies researcher, Dr. Julia T. Wood, explains that we need to pay attention to nonverbal behaviors because they account for 65%-93% of the total meaning of a message. According to Wood, nonverbal communication tends to be perceived as more credible because most of us think that nonverbal communication is more trustworthy when it comes to expressing true emotions.

- Hand Gestures
- Eye Contact or Avoidance
- Lack of Smile
- Silence
- Hand & Arm Placement
- Body Gesture
- Postures
- Physical Touch
- Personal Zone

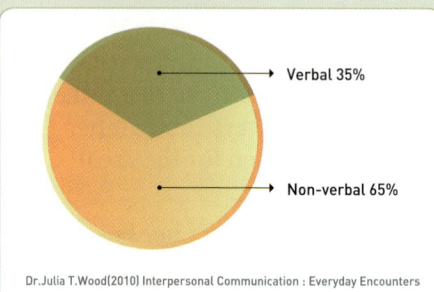

Dr.Julia T.Wood(2010) Interpersonal Communication : Everyday Encounters

4. Role Plays

Read each situation and role play with your partner.

01 Situation Your boss will be out of town this Friday, and he wants you to run a conference call. You are a bit nervous to conduct a phone meeting because it is your first time to make a conference call overseas in English. Discuss with your team members appropriate global conference call manners and etiquette along with cultural differences.

02 Situation You are visiting your clients in the US to attend meetings. After the last meeting, the client invites you to dinner. Ask some questions about different dining manners and cultural differences.

03 Situation You are giving a presentation in a global conference in Germany. Now you are taking questions after you're done presenting. You are aware that Germans tend to be straightforward and do not like idle talk. You'd like to get to the point quickly like Germans generally do during the Q & A session. How can you deal with some personal or completely unrelated questions?

5. Discussion

Discuss the following questions in detail.

1. Is it normal to turn to people or walk up to them and introduce yourself in your country?

2. When giving a business card, what's the first step for you to take? Do you read it carefully and make comments before putting it away?

3. Is it considered acceptable for people to interrupt each other when talking in your country?

4. In your culture, how close do you stand to people when you are talking to them? Demonstrate the distance.

5. Understanding cultural differences in nonverbal communications is also essential. Talk with your partners about personal experiences of nonverbal communications (e.g. nodding [yes/no], pointing to an object, or pointing with one finger, etc.)

One Point Lesson

Come vs. Go

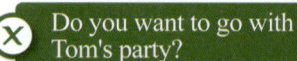
Do you want to go with me to Tom's party?

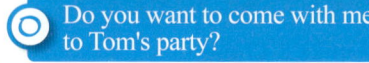
Do you want to come with me to Tom's party?

Go and come both show movement, but these words are used differently, depending on the situation and on the locations of the person speaking and the person being addressed.
"Come" is used for movement toward the place where the speaker is, was, or intends to be, or toward the person being talked about. We could say, "Why didn't he come to see us?" "Go" is used for movement in other directions.

Here is one example.

[Situation] Brad is in the living room. Angelina is in the kitchen.

Angelina: Dinner's ready!
Brad: Okay, I'm coming!

LESSON 15 / Different Communication Styles 75

6. Business Skills - Understanding Different Communication Styles

When traveling overseas, it's important to learn the culture and how to communicate. It's very easy to be misunderstood and lose the client and the company's business. You should do research and discover the way to follow another country's culture and customs.

A Business vocabulary

Discuss these words and their meanings to understand business vocabulary.

1. Cause offense:
2. Open to misinterpretation:
3. Nod:
4. Keep still:
5. Latecomers:
6. Frown upon:
7. Unnerve:
8. Temper tantrums:
9. Eye contact:

B Mistakes in communication

For each situation, describe what the problem is and how to correct it.
Use the vocabulary above to discuss scenarios

Example: During negotiations with a potential customer from Japan, Michael said "no" to several important propositions. It has been two weeks now, and he hasn't heard anything. He is worried that the potential client has decided to use one of his competitors.

Answer: Michael might lose the deal. The potential client may have been offended. In Japan, "no" is considered an impolite word. Michael should have learned something about the culture in order to be better prepared for the meeting.

01 Andrew, a representative for an **American** manufacturing company, had arranged an important meeting in Rio with a group of **Brazilian** businessmen to discuss their possible investment in his company's new business plan. When the Brazilians arrived at the conference room, Andrew had been waiting for them for 15 minutes.

What's the problem?

02 Mark is an engineer from **Scotland**. He was 10 minutes late for an important meeting with a potential client in Amsterdam. Mark's company is well-known and can offer better prices than his competitors. However, now the **Dutch** client isn't replying to his follow-up e-mails.

What's the problem?

03 Jack is a cell phone distributer from **Korea**. He's in **Russia** to start a new distributorship. The sales manager he's meeting with begins to get very angry and is starting to hit the table. Jack's face turns red, and he quickly agrees with the price the Russian manager wants. As he's leaving, the manager says, "It was nice to meet you, but I won't do business with you."

What's the problem?

Wrapping Up!

▶ 3 new words from this lesson

▶ 3 new expressions from this lesson

▶ 3 things to remember

Lesson 16

Global Business Success

Learning Objective

After completing this lesson, you will be able to...
- talk about global brands and the factors to succeed in the globalized market.
- discuss the close relationship between understanding cultures and doing business internationally.

OVERVIEW
☐ Warm Up Activities
☐ Useful Expressions
☐ Dialogue
☐ Language Practice
☐ Business Basics
☐ Role Plays
☐ Discussion
☐ One Point Lesson
☐ Business Skills

1. Warm Up Activities

A Discuss the following questions with a partner.

1. Which global brands do well in your country, and which do not?
2. What is your favorite global brand, and why?
3. What is one major difference between global and local brands? Give specific examples.

B Today's situation

Look at the situation and role play with your classmates.

"Interview with Global Leaders"

Liz Claman asks Alex Gorsky about the key factors for success in the industry.

Alex Gorsky: The CEO of the Johnson & Johnson Legacy
Liz Claman: CNBC's reporter, interviews one of the world's most successful CEOs

Useful Expressions

A Closed Questions
- Are you feeling better today?
- Is the prime rib a special tonight?
- Did that man walk by the house before?
- Can I help you with that?
- Have you used our product before?

B Open Questions
- What happened at the meeting?
- Why did he react that way?
- How was the party?
- What did you get up to on vacation?
- What else do we need to do?

C Today's Expressions

Match the expressions (1-5) with the similar meanings (a-e).

① We've met on a number of occasions.
② I don't know what the future holds for us.
③ We should find out what they truly want.
④ He talks tough, but he always caves in when someone disagrees with him.
⑤ The competition in this industry is pretty cut-throat.

☐ a. He sounds like he has a strong spirit, but he easily gives in.
☐ b. I met up with him for several reasons.
☐ c. We don't know what we'll be doing a year from now.
☐ d. We should try to see things from their perspective.
☐ e. It's a dog-eat-dog-world.

LESSON 16 / Global Business Success 77

2. Dialogue
Read the dialogue and answer the questions with a partner.

How to Grow Your Business Globally

Liz What are the factors that led Johnson & Johnson to become a successful global brand?

Alex There are a number of factors, but when you get down to brass tacks, the main one is to truly understand the global needs. We always try to put ourselves in our customers' shoes and find out what they truly want from us.

Liz I see. What else is the key to becoming a successful, top-notch brand?

Alex Being just a good observer isn't good enough for us. The products should be the best of the best, the cream of the crop. The competition in this industry is pretty cut-throat.

Liz That's for sure. Have you ever caved under pressure, thinking by the time a new product launches, things might go wrong?

Alex Yes, to customers, sometimes your best isn't good enough. In order to become the world's best brands, they should always be perfect. I don't know what the future holds for us, but our mission is still to bring the most satisfying products to the world.

Comprehension Questions
Q1. Who is Alex Gorsky?
Q2. What is the interviewer's first question?
Q3. According to Alex Gorsky, what is the most essential factor to become one of the global market leaders?
Q4. What did he mean when he said, "Sometimes your best isn't good enough"?

3. Language Practice

A Chunks & Chew
Complete the sentences with the appropriate words and expressions from the dialogue.

☐ get down to brass tracks
☐ a top-notch
☐ the cream of the crop
☐ cut-throat
☐ go wrong

① Companies like that put a lot of effort in recruiting _____.
② Law school competition is as _____ as its reputation.
③ The relationship started to _____ when they moved abroad.
④ We've wasted too much time on chatting. Let's _____.
⑤ The most important aspect of giving _____ presentation is to be prepared.

B Key Patterns
Here are some key patterns that you can use when talking about global business success.

① **By the time** _____.
- he finished the first project, he had received a huge paycheck
- you are done working, I will already be gone
- he's up and ready, all the best food will be gone

② **Have you ever** _____?
- been late for work
- worked for a fortune 500 company
- called in sick to work

③ _____ be/be not + adjective **enough** _____.
- The actor isn't tough / to play "the boss"
- Sometimes my co-worker is hard on herself for not being productive enough
- It was good / for government work

Business Basics

Ways to Build Cultural Intelligence (CQ)

"Cultural Intelligence" (CQ) is a concept that incorporates the ability to interact effectively across global cultures and diverse workplaces. Here are some practical ways to increase your "cultural intelligence" when working abroad:

- ☐ Approach everyone as an individual–don't make assumptions based on a group identity.
- ☐ Understand that cultural tendencies such as mannerisms are not necessarily indicators of a person's performance and capabilities.
- ☐ Seek feedback to confirm the other person understood what you were really communicating.
- ☐ Reconfirm your understanding by paraphrasing what you have read or heard.
- ☐ Stay away from using jargons and metaphors defined by your own cultural background.
- ☐ Listen to silence–it means different things in different cultures!
- ☐ Find a cultural informant/interpreter to coach or guide you.
- ☐ Use pictures, diagrams, or stories to convey your messages.
- ☐ Make an attempt to learn the logic behind the new culture–the connection between appearances, behaviors, and values.
- ☐ Take part in intercultural training in the new location to gain insights into how your foreign counterparts communicate and behave.

4. Role Plays

Read each situation and role play with your partner.

• 01 Situation

You are the marketing manager of a large Italian company, and you are organizing an event in Japan. You are launching a new product and have invited some senior directors and VIPs to the event. Your designer placed white flowers all around the exhibition area, and later you found out white flowers are a symbol of death in Japan. Ask your group partners for some advice.

• 02 Situation

You are the owner of an agency, and you are just about to call it a night. Just before you leave, the phone starts to ring. It is after midnight, and everyone's gone home. You answer it and find out the person needs your help urgently. What would you tell the person if you were a major global leader?

• 03 Situation

You are launching a new low-cost airline overseas. You need to hire top management. You will need a CFO and a CMO who are willing to work and live in a foreign country. Have a short meeting with a headhunter/consultant who will help you recruit your team.

5. Discussion

Discuss the following questions in detail.

1. What could be the most important factors affecting global CEOs over the next three years?
2. What are the characteristics that all top global brands have in common?
3. How can a local brand become a global brand? Name some examples.
4. Do global brands benefit from a unique worldwide image?
5. Check out the top 10 global brands this year. What do they provide to consumers?

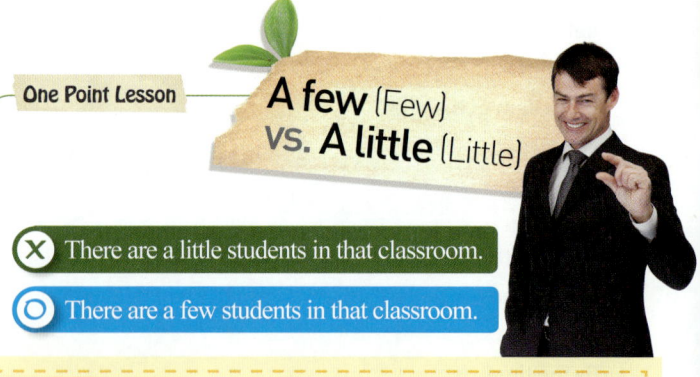

One Point Lesson — A few (Few) vs. A little (Little)

✗ There are a little students in that classroom.
◎ There are a few students in that classroom.

"A few" is used with plural countable nouns, like cars, chairs, people, etc. "A little" is used with uncountable nouns, like water, wine, traffic, and so on.

"Little" and "few" convey a negative meaning. For example, we use "little" to mean "not much, not enough." The speaker is unhappy about it. However, we use "a little" to mean "not much but enough." It means that the speaker is okay with it.

LESSON 16 / Global Business Success

6. Business Skills - Global Brands & Success

To be a successful global brand requires building an image and a relationship with many international markets. Each corporation must address the cultural problems and difficulties to sell their products and services in order to have an effective presence around the world. In order to create a successful brand, many factors must be in place.

A. What makes a global brand successful

As a group, brainstorm what is necessary to be successful. The following list includes ideas that should be addressed. Why are these points important? What are some important global brands that you can think of? What do they have in common?

- ☐ Create an exciting name or symbol.
- ☐ Discuss the problem of associating it with a specific country.
- ☐ Consider cultural tastes and differences.
- ☐ Develop attractive packaging.
- ☐ Address environmental and social pressures
- ☐ Discuss how to deal with government legislation that is different from country to country
- ☐ Consider the price as it relates to each different country

B. Global brands – Coca-Cola

Choose the correct word from the word box. Fill in the blanks.

Word Box	tops, success, giant, catchy, beverages, rival, inspire, partners, known

The Coca-Cola Company is a soft drink ①_____ that was established in 1886. Its mission is "to strive to refresh the world, ②_____ moments of optimism and happiness, create value and make a difference." It often ③_____ the list of being the world's most recognizable brand. Its iconic Coca Cola drink, also ④_____ as Coke, started life as medicine. Today, it is one of the biggest selling products on the planet. The company website says its 3,300+ ⑤_____ are sold in over 200 countries. It sells 1.6 billion drinks a day and employs close to 100,000 people. One secret to the company's phenomenal ⑥_____ is what it calls the "Coca-Cola system" – the more than 300 worldwide bottling ⑦_____ that work together to distribute its products. Another is its ⑧_____ advertising slogans, such as "Coke Is It." Its biggest ⑨_____ is Pepsi.

① Write all the words you can think of about Coca-Cola on the board or on a piece of paper. Talk about these words with your partner(s).

② Writes down a pretend rumor about Coca-Cola. Walk around the class and talk to other students about their rumor.

③ Brainstorm good and bad things about Coca-Cola and write them on the board. Then, talk about these in pairs.

Wrapping Up!

▶ 3 new words from this lesson

▶ 3 new expressions from this lesson

▶ 3 things to remember

Business Practice 1

04 Embrace Diversity

CASE STUDY 04

◉ Background

ChevronTexaco is the world's fourth largest publicly-traded energy company and an international leader in finding, producing and marketing oil and gas. Active in more than 180 countries, the company's Caltex, Texaco and Chevron branded products hold top-tier rankings worldwide. Its business extends beyond producing and refining chemicals through Chevron Phillips Co., which has interests in 30 power projects now operating or being developed across five continents.

For Chevron, diversity and inclusion mean going beyond acceptance of cultural, ethnic, national or religious differences. They value and encourage diversity in their employees' thoughts and personal views.

[*"We learn from and respect the cultures in which we work. We value and demonstrate respect for the uniqueness of individuals and the varied perspectives and talents they provide. We have an inclusive work environment and actively embrace a diversity of people, ideas, talents and experiences."*]

Chevron believes that the quality of their diversity improves the work environment. Their commitment to diversity is more than words, more than a set of goals. Their actions speak for themselves. Chevron's philosophy is that the diversity of thinking helps bring about better solutions; whether the diversity is in technical backgrounds, geographic backgrounds or gender backgrounds, people look at problems different ways.

◉ Diversity

Read the following information and answer the questions.

> Approximately 25,000 Chevron employees participate in one or more specialized training and networking groups. These groups focus on gender, race, sexual orientation, age, disability and nationality. These networks help improve communication among employees and cultivate links to the communities where the employees work.
>
> Diversity councils throughout the company help promote a work environment which helps to provide every employee with the maximum opportunity to contribute to company goals. They ensure employees understand company policies and demonstrate employees are included with programs such as diversity training, diversity moments, personal diversity action plans and lunch-time diversity learning sessions.

- What does "diversity" mean?
- How many employees participate in diversity training groups?
- How does networking help the employees?
- What do these groups focus on?
- What do the diversity councils do for the employees?
- Why do you think this is important for the employees? The company?

CASE STUDY 04

◉ Analyze

Look at the chart below. Check which diversity topics are most important to you. Which of the items change how you communicate with someone? Work in pairs to discuss the different ways you speak to someone because of the areas that you checked.

1	Age	
2	Gender	
3	Race	
4	Ethnicity	
5	Religion	
6	Geographic Location	
7	Occupation	
8	Different Socioeconomic Status	
9	Educational Background	
10	Appearance (skin color included)	
11	Parental Status	
12	Marital Status	
13	Ethical Values	
14	Treatment of Elders	
15	Relationship to Authority	
16	Language Differences (accents included)	

◉ Presentation _ Planning Cross-Cultural Training

01 Work in small groups. You are a member of the HR management of Chevron. Brainstorm ideas of how to plan the diversity training and suggest the best programs for your employees.

02 Deliver a presentation to the other teams and choose the best one.

◉ Writing

Your company has just merged with a global company. There are many new employees in the company from many parts of the world. The new employees aren't aware of many cultural rules of your country. The other employees are getting very upset, and it's causing work to slow down, putting your company behind schedule. You are the manager, and you need to get everyone back on track.

Write an e-mail addressed to everyone on how to improve relations between employees as well as instruct international employees on business etiquette in the office.

Dear Employees,

I want to take this opportunity to welcome our new international staff. We are a new team, and understanding each other can be a challenge. For this reason, it's important to clearly outline office protocol so we can all work well together.
First, let me explain ……

HOW OPEN ARE YOU TO DIVERSITY?

Rate each statement below on a scale of 1 to 5 in how it describes you currently.

1 = Strongly agree. This describes me well.
2 = Mildly agree. This describes me most of the time.
3 = Agree. This describes me sometimes but not all the time.
4 = Disagree. This is usually NOT my behavior most of the time.
5 = Strongly disagree. This is definitely NOT me. I do not do this.

	Statement	Score
1	I feel comfortable about meeting internationals (foreign nationals) or those culturally different for the first time.	1 2 3 4 5
2	I am skilled and patient at dealing with someone who speaks your language as a second language and has limited speaking ability.	1 2 3 4 5
3	I actively seek out opportunities to interact with people of other cultures at meetings, conferences and social events.	1 2 3 4 5
4	I am currently involved in learning a new language and/or culture.	1 2 3 4 5
5	I enjoy exploring new restaurants, movies or cultural events of cultures and ethnic origins other than my own.	1 2 3 4 5
6	I admit my own stereotypes and prejudices about other groups and seek to increase my understanding.	1 2 3 4 5
7	I create and seek out friendship, colleagueship or arrangements with people who are culturally different from me.	1 2 3 4 5
8	I belong to a professional or social group where the membership is very diverse.	1 2 3 4 5
9	I understand how cultural factors impact the way people communicate and relate. (In business, I understand how culture impacts the sales, marketing, management style and customer service of my company/services and those of my customers from other countries.)	1 2 3 4 5
10	I understand and can comfortably handle (competently manage) the differences in communication styles, protocols, gift giving and greetings in at least one culture/country other than my own.	1 2 3 4 5

Questions for Discussion:

- Which of these statements has the highest score? ....
- Which of these statements has the lowest score? ....
- What's your average score? Compare with your partner. ....

Business Practice 1
Answer Key

ANSWER KEY — Business Practice 1

Unit 1. People & Relationships

Lesson 01

Chunks & Chew

① extensive experience
② targeted demographics
③ bottom line
④ collaborating with
⑤ hit the ground running

Lesson 02

Useful Expressions

1-b, 2-d, 3-a, 4-c

Chunks & Chew

① catching up on
② Check out
③ brief / on
④ fallen behind on
⑤ keep / posted

Business Skills

1) Showing Interest
* Uh-huh. I understand.
* That sounds interesting!
* Really?

2) Finding Common Areas
* Neither do I.
* Absolutely. I agree.
* So do I.

3) Further Questions
* How did you feel?
* So, what happened to you?
* Then, what did you do next?

4) Echoing Interesting Facts
* All over the country?
* Born in England?
* Three thousand?

Lesson 03

Useful Expressions

1-c, 2-d, 3-b, 4-a

Chunks & Chew

① pressed for
② crunched the numbers
③ bean counters
④ right off the bat
⑤ on a health kick

Business Skills

A. Dictionary of Formal & Informal English

* About ⇒ Regarding, Concerning
* And ⇒ As well as, Moreover, Besides
* Because ⇒ Due to
* But ⇒ While, Whereas
* Get in touch ⇒ Contact
* Enough ⇒ Sufficient
* Thanks ⇒ I appreciate…
* Sorry ⇒ We regret…

B. Rewrite the Sentences

a. How about dinner Saturday?
   ⇒ Would it be possible to meet this Saturday for dinner?

b. See you at the conference next Monday!
   ⇒ I look forward to seeing you at the conference on Monday.

c. I want to have a meeting with you sometime next week.
   ⇒ Please let me know if you are available to meet sometime next week.

d. You can call me any time.
   ⇒ Please feel free to call me anytime if you have questions or concerns.

e. I want to visit your new office. Is that okay?
   ⇒ I am interested in touring your new office. Would that be possible?

f. I can't come to the trade fair next Monday. I'm busy.
   ⇒ I will be unable to attend next Monday's sales conference due to a previous engagement.

Lesson 04

Useful Expressions

1-c, 2-a, 3-d, 4-b

Chunks & Chew

① get / on the horn
② pick back up
③ fret over
④ speak of the devil
⑤ get assistance from

Business Skills

A. Tim-related Expressions

① behind schedule
② ahead of time
③ in the nick of time
④ be pressed for time
⑤ on time

ANSWER KEY 85

Unit 2. Company & Business

Lesson 05

Useful Expressions

1-a, 2-b, 3-d, 4-c

Chunks & Chew

① get / perks
② flexible hours
③ bumped into
④ landed / job
⑤ pay hikes

Business Skills

A. Categorizing

* Introduction: 2, 5, 6, 10
* Body: 3, 7, 11, 12
* Conclusion: 1, 4, 8, 9

Lesson 06

Useful Expressions

1-c, 2-a, 3-e, 4-d, 5-b

Chunks & Chew

① be set for
② swing by
③ works against
④ butting in
⑤ talk over

Business Skills

A. Matching Words that describe work hours and facilities

A-4, B-10, C-5, D-6, E-11, F-9, G-8, H-1, I-3, J-2, K-7

B. Discussing business and personal time balance

① night shift
② day shift
③ full time
④ freelance
⑤ overtime
⑥ sick pay
⑦ office hours
⑧ vacation
⑨ break room
⑩ smoking area
⑪ cubicle

Lesson 07

Useful Expressions

1-e, 2-d, 3-a. 4-b, 5-c

Chunks & Chew

① short-handed
② have a point
③ break the rules
④ up to our necks
⑤ get back to

Business Skills

2) Practice

* Carved in stone: inflexible, permanent
* Underdressing: wearing very informal or casual clothes
* Corporate culture: business world
* Button-down: very conservative, traditional
* Slovenly: messy, dirty, careless
* Upward-bound: aspiring to be in management

Lesson 08

Useful Expressions

1-b, 2-c, 3-e, 4-d, 5-a

Chunks & Chew

① bring / to
② pulled together
③ work on
④ get over the hump
⑤ called into question

Business Skills

01. Vocabulary used to describe brands

* Positive: superior, exceptional, merits, value, attributes excellent, worth

* Neutral: characteristics, properties, status, choice, select, quality, features

* Negative: disadvantage, hitch, faults, wrinkle, downfall, barrier, hindrance, impediment, obstacle, defect, hurdle, flaw, shortcomings

ANSWER KEY — Business Practice 1

Unit 3. Communicating in Business

Lesson 09

Useful Expressions

1-b, 2-a, 3-c, 4-d

Chunks & Chew

① To my knowledge
② picks up
③ put me through
④ get a spare moment
⑤ not handy

Business Skills

A. Leaving a Message

e) (1) What have you been up to?
i) (2) Are you staying busy?
c) (3) What can I do for you today?
a) (4) Is he available?
h) (5) Can I put you on hold? I'll see if he is in.
f) (6) I'm afraid he is not at his desk.
b) (7) Would you like to call back or leave a message?
d) (8) Will do.
g) (9) Looking forward to it.

Lesson 10

Useful Expressions

1-c, 2-d, 3-a, 4-b

Chunks & Chew

① push / back to
② take place
③ Apart from
④ confirm / with
⑤ give / a rundown

Business Skills

A. Scheduling a Meeting

(1) 3:30 is good. Does that work for you?
(2) Next week sounds good, say Tuesday at 3? What do you think?
(3) Tuesday at 10 is best for me. Is that good for you?
(4) 1 o'clock at my office. That works for me.
(5) No, I'm afraid Monday's out. What about Friday?
(6) How about 2 o'clock on Friday? What do you think?

Lesson 11

Useful Expressions

1-e, 2-a, 3-c, 4-b, 5-d

Chunks & Chew

① come up with
② hammer / out
③ called a meeting
④ shaping up
⑤ a ballpark figure

Business Skills

A. Categorizing

* Clarifying a point: 7, 8, 9
* Offering a different opinion: 1, 2, 3
* Politely disagreeing: 4, 5, 6
* Interrupting: 10, 11, 12

B. Direct vs. Indirect Communication

1. I don't think that's a good idea.
- Do you think that's a good idea?
- Are there any other ideas?
- I like most parts of that idea.

2. That's not the point.
- That's an interesting point.
- That's another good point.

3. I think we should do (something)
- I have one possible suggestion.
- What do you think of this idea?

4. Those figures are not accurate.
- I have some other figures here.
- Those figures may be slightly old.

5. You're doing that wrong.
- I would do that like this.
- Have you tried doing that this way?

6. I don't agree.
- I have another idea.
- What do you think of this idea?
- May I make a suggestion?

Lesson 12

Useful Expressions

1-b, 2-d, 3-a, 4-c

Chunks & Chew

① cut out for
② take a rain check
③ toot / horn
④ up-and-coming
⑤ pan out

ANSWER KEY

Business Skills

A. Common E-mail Vocabulary

1. attachment
2. appreciate
3. know
4. request
5. ASAP
6. satisfactory
7. inquire
8. interest
9. send
10. received

B. Formal and informal e-mail phrases

* Requesting Information:
  4. Please answer ASAP.
  1. Can you help?
  8. Can you send me…?

* Replies: 5, 6, 3, 2, 7, 8
  5. I'm sending you the … in an attachment.
  6. I'm sending you….
  3. Let us know if you need any more help.
  2. We hope you are happy with us.
  7. We are working on your request….

Unit 4. Cross-Cultural Relations

Lesson 13

Useful Expressions

1-b, 2-c, 3-d, 4-a

Chunks & Chew

① put / down
② snowed under with
③ in a jiffy
④ acting on
⑤ filed away

Business Skills

B. Meeting New Clients

1-b, 2-b, 3-c, 4-c&d, 5-b, 6-b, 7-b

Lesson 14

Useful Expressions

1-b, 2-d, 3-a, 4-c

Chunks & Chew

① make mistakes
② in advance
③ brush up on
④ put in charge of
⑤ give advice

Business Skills

B. Cultural Diversity

1) Verbal Communication: Japan
2) Gestures: Greeks
3) Physical Touch: Thailand
4) At a Restaurant: China, Sweden, China

Lesson 15

Useful Expressions

1-b, 2-d, 3-a, 4-e, 5-c

Chunks & Chew

① have faith in
② widened our horizons
③ playing favorites
④ bummed out
⑤ a pain in the neck

Lesson 16

Useful Expressions

1-b, 2-c, 3-d, 4-a, 5-e

Chunks & Chew

① the cream of the crop
② cut-throat
③ go wrong
④ get down to brass tracks
⑤ a top-notch

Business Skills

B. Global Brands - Coca-Cola

(1) giant
(2) inspire
(3) tops
(4) know
(5) beverages
(6) success
(7) partners
(8) catchy
(9) rival